Joy in Simplicity

Joy in Simplicity

Embracing Minimalism for a Happier Life

Evelyn Hartwell

Mindful Pages

Published in 2024

ISBN: 9789362923059 (PB)
ISBN: 9789362920096 (eBook)

Published by

Mindful Pages
Imprint of Alpha Editions LLC
312 W. 2nd St #1834
Casper, WY 82601, USA
www.mindfulpagespublishers.com

All rights reserved. No part of this publication may be reproduced, distributed, or transmitted in any form or by any means, including photocopying, recording, or other electronic or mechanical methods, without the prior written permission of the publisher, except in the case of brief quotations embodied in critical reviews and specific other non-commercial uses permitted by copyright law.

Table of Contents

Introduction

Life is by its very nature simple and never was inherently complicated. But today's living conditions are so complicated that it seems it hides the simplicity within us, by heaping our life with physical and mental clutter. I can still hear the resonating echo of times when my life was in complete disarray. I had so much on my plate that I had endless to-do lists, my house was a depository for the things I hardly used, and I had the burden of incessant demands of modern life. It was during this overwhelming stage of my life that I realized that I was desiring to experience life in a different and simpler way. I wanted a quiet, peaceful, and joyful life.

The breakthrough of my transformation was due to a deep introspection period. After that reflection, I came to question what was really worth of the position in my life and therefore of my rubbers, the commitments which was I devoted to and the constant demand for more that governed my life. It was like I have been in a race without a definite halting point; a race that made me tired and not elated. This self-examination showed me that minimalism was not only a remedy that was enough for now but also was a lesson which promised me a deeper sense of inner peace and contentment.

From my point of view, minimalism implies much more than merely the rejection of all the stuff in excess. It is a purposeful resolve to focus on what is really important, distinction from the non-essential, and to create space—both physical and mental—for what causes genuine happiness. In a culture where material possession is often seen as a sign of achievement and that is the only route to success, minimalism is a bold imperative: the argument that a lot less can, indeed, be more.

A life of minimalism should start with a shift in point of view. It calls us to redefine our needs and discard the non-necessities that are holding us back. So, this is not a period of hardship but a phase of freedom. Absolutely we are the ones who release ourselves from the mess that keeps us from the very things that are sincerely significant to us—love, creativity, and self-care.

Living simply has a compelling potential. When we remove the things that distract us and pull us away in all different directions, we realize that we have more time and energy to spend on the things that make us happy. This could be the extra time spent with your family, an out-of-the-ordinary leisure activity the kids have taken up, or the authentic peace one gets from a neat and clean home. Whichever mode it is, the core of minimalism is all about improving the quality of our lives through the choices we make.

At therapy, I was introduced to a very fundamental truth: "Contentment is not a product to be bought but a state to be lived." Happiness is not about the things we can buy but a permanent measure of peace that we are in. Being able to make conscious decisions, creating social bonds, and the peaceful feeling when we have enough are the sources of real happiness. The philosophy of minimalism is like an order of the day that purposes to disentangle ourselves and enjoy the already existing prosperity we have but we can hardly perceive of because of the unnecessary clutter of our world.

After being initiated into the Wabi-Sabi lifestyle by heading towards a simpler life, one must set intentions that are clear and precise. What exactly are you after in your quest for minimalism? Might the peace that arises from a simpler life be on top of your list or the desire to concentrate more on personal growth be the main thing? Regardless of your wants, staying mindful of these objectives will act as a rudder to your life and get you to the most fulfilling.

In my personal example, the act of setting intentions has had a huge impact on my life. It has allowed me to look at minimalism in a new way, not as a list of rules I have to follow, but as my personal journey which is exclusively mine. Through concentrating on the actual objectives that give rise to a happier, more peaceful, simpler life, I have come up with decisions that stand up to these purposes, rather than falling into the pitfalls of not abiding by this or the other minimalist design.

Minimalism is not a stop but an end. The process goes on, and it is all about examining our desires, perfecting the list of things that constitute the essence of our lives, and making changes as things develop over time. At present it is incentivizing it that is the point where it gets really difficult because you simply cannot get out of the consumerist trap, or the grind of daily life seems the biggest obstacle. In such cases, what plays well is revisiting your intentions, recalling the reasons you walked this path, and being sure that the benefits of simplicity are way more than the temporary discomfort of giving up.

In composing this text, it is my aim to not only teach minimalism as a means of gaining a human being of detachment but also to re-awaken the joy of freedom that comes from the experience of living with less. The world we encounter is intricate and quite often dizzying, however, we can find easier ways to deal with our management of the world by adopting the principle of simplicity in our life. This is the assurance of minimalism—a life of joy in simplicity, where happiness is not a goal to be pursued, but a natural byproduct of living in harmony with our true selves.

While reading through this book, try to be mindful of what minimalism can teach you, which is giving joy and peace. It may not always be a comfortable ride, but I believe it is the most important thing one can do in life. Empowered by simplicity, we are not simply making our lives less complicated. We are getting back our time, energy, and happiness. By making these changes, we are allowing ourselves to fill our lives with what truly matters - the difference between living a simple life or living a life with purpose.

Chapter 1

The Philosophy of Minimalism

Minimalism, the term which is generally understood as the modern response to the overconsumption of goods and a fast pace of life in the present day, has its origin in the thoughts of philosophical thinking. One can begin to really get to know one's minimalistic self when one transcends the superficial ideas of simplicity and decluttering and instead of that, one starts to study the philosophical thoughts that have over the years proclaimed the values of an intentional and purposeful life. This chapter aims to investigate the ancient and continuous philosophy of minimalism, searching back to the earliest sources in wisdom of old, looking at its transformation in the modern world, and comparing it to the existing consumeristic culture. The intersection thus caused will unveil what are the links between minimalism and how one lives in accordance with their most deeply held values.

At first, one usually gets the hint of minimalism when he starts with dissatisfaction—a hint that he will relationships that do not bring us happiness and satisfaction. This is not a revelation exclusively to our time. Since the beginning of humanity, philosophers have been brooding on what shapes attraction, contentment, and a good life. From the Stoics of ancient Greece to the wise persons of the East, simplicity and moderation have been asserted as the main qualities of a good life. These thinkers saw that the true source of happiness is not in the accumulation of luxury and property but in the discovery of inner peace and the pursuit of the most fundamental things.

The Stoic philosophers of ancient Greece saw life in a different way, and their ideas were concerned with the importance of self-discipline, rationality, and harmony with the universe. Such as Seneca and Epictetus beings of the external dimension- whether it be material wealth or social status or physical comfort- are not really our own well-being. They are the ones who wrote that the important thing is the state of our mind and the extent to which we live in accordance with our rational nature. Stoics' internal virtues over external wealth is one of the first signs of minimalism: a focus on the essentials, a rejection of excess, and a dedication to live with purposes.

Somewhat identically in the East, the concept of Aparigraha, a Sanskrit word that is usually translated as non-possessiveness or non-greed, is a major elaboration of Jainism and Hinduism. Aparigraha is a calling for minimal possessions, the ending of desire, and getting off of material wealth. However, this is not all about renunciation just for the sake of it. It is also about creating the mental and spiritual space which is crucial for the pursuit of a purposeful life and a deeper sense of life awareness. Among the Buddhists who also uphold the philosophy of simplicity, is regarded as a way to enlightenment. By lowering dependence on material goods and focusing on the present moment, people can escape the suffering brought about by craving and desire.

These age-old philosophies are the stepping stones on the way of understanding the real meaning of minimalism. They justify that apparently the quest for a simpler life is not necessarily the only way to unclutter our homes but to declutter our minds and souls as well. It is the elimination of the extraneous so that we can solely drop attention down to the really essential things. This means that minimalism is not a new distinction but actually, an everlasting principle that has been advocated by some of the greatest intellects in human history.

As we move into the modern era, minimalism is more prevalent in various forms and interpretations, reflecting the modern lifestyle's special challenges and opportunities. The 20th-century industrial revolution and the increase of consumer culture accompanied the unhindered spread of products and services. For the first time in history, large numbers of people were able to choose from a practically limitless number of items, which undoubtedly promised to make their lives easier, more comfortable, and more joyful. However, this abundance was accompanied by an increased dissatisfaction because people discovered they were trapped in a pattern of endless consumption, perpetually wanting more but never really achieving inner peace.

As a response to this, a new form of minimalist living was born which is characterized by the refusal of consumer culture and a comeback to the values of minimalism and intentional life. This new minimalism is not just about having less stuff; it is about being the master of your destiny. It is about the decisions, we make with regard to how we use our time, our energy, and our belongings, and especially it is about choosing the things that are truly meaningful to us. In other words, minimalism becomes a tool which serves as a source of personal power empowering us to live truly and authentically when so much around us is otherwise.

The diversity minimalism exhibits is probably the most surprising features of modern minimalism. While the utmost principles such as focusing on the essentials, avoiding excess, and the notion of minimalism as a choice to live one's life are the same, the interpretations and applications of these principles might be widely differing. For example, minimalism can be to live in a small house, which contains only necessities and gadgets might be considered to be particularly extreme when it comes to commitment. Others might want to free up their time by canceling nonessential appointments and spending time with a close group of friends only. In the age of technology, the idea of minimalism has taken on yet another twist as people decide to limit their exposure to screens, downsize their digital footprint, and maybe suspend the communication and information they receive.

At the core, minimalism is moral living. It is based on the idea of recognizing that we are all limited beings, we have only a certain number of hours of life and the manner in which we choose to use time and our energy resources will determine how good a life we will have. In a world that usually overestimates the quantity of anything while diminishing the quality of many things, minimalism offers a better option: the fact that less can be more, that one can enrich his/her life by focusing on vital issues. However, minimalism and consumerism are two antagonistic worldviews that are found to be prevalent. Consumerism is a culture that insinuates to us the idea that we can buy happiness and that the secret of a satisfactory life is to stock up on wealth, possessions, and status. However, many people have come to realize that the pathway of more is a voyage that causes even excessive amounts of stress, anxiety, and an idea of emptiness. Minimalism breaks this pattern of lifestyle by contending that being joyful is not about having but rather about needing less. Shifting our gaze to experiences rather than material objects which act as the building blocks for the purpose of our life—our relationships, our passions, and our personal growth—we can achieve a deeper, more enduring sense of fulfillment.

Finally, minimalism essentially means making a choice with a purpose in one's life. It asks us to reflect on the things we have been taught about what a successful life is and to wonder if there can be a better, simpler way. It compels us to refuse the excessive, to reject the noise, and to focus on what is truly essential. By doing that, we can create a space where we have the freedom to enjoy those supporting aspects of the living experience that give us delight, meaning, and a mission to live for. In this space, we can strive to respect the true art of living—through simple living, mindfulness, and intentionality.

Simplicity Through the Ages

Given that the world is a place full of varying living beings and things, the simple-attract-option has long captivated the minds of philosophers and thinkers across centuries. In the present day, minimalism is often seen as the modern way of living, which shifts away from the excessive consumerism and infatuation with technology we face in the 21st century. However, the nature of minimalism, in the philosophical view, is much deeper, and it originated in ancient traditions, which have been familiar with living with a clear intent and purpose. The study of these ancient philosophies will give us an insight into the timeless nature of minimalism and its relevance to this fast modern society.

The ancient Stoic philosophers of Greece and Rome are some of the earliest and most influential examples of the framework of minimalist thinking. Central to Stoicism is the tenets that happiness and contentedness are not derivable from external things but one's interior. The Stoics believed that the key to a good life lies in the development of inner virtues, such as wisdom, courage, and self-control, and in the concentration on the things we can control with the simultaneous realization of the idea that there are things that we cannot control.

One of the major Stoic philosophers-Seneca-aimed to draw the stern and simple side of life besides the harmful excess of the wealth era. Seneca in his letters and essays, often warned against the pursuit of material goods, insisting that such activities usually result in more anxiety than satisfaction. He was of the opinion that through the reduction of our desires, and the acceptance of the reality that we have so learns to be pleased with such things, we can live a life more peacefully and fully. For Seneca, the epitome of simplicity is not the denial of life's joys, but the removal of the barriers that keep the truly important virtues in our lives out of sight, e.g.. personal growth, relationships, and inner tranquillity.

Concerning morality and ethical behavior, it was the Stoic philosopher Epictetus who pointed out as well that the wise person keeps the emphasis on one's internal locus of control and lets go of the irrational and harmful to the sanity of individuals such as grief, anger or fear. According to him, people generally concern themselves about types of wealth, some of which are numbers, belongings, and physical comfort that they cannot finally get as they are beyond human control and thus can't be the object of their anxiety.

Besides, he told this disciple, they should turn to the world in a different way, focusing on the work on their own character and becoming more natural. The theory of another Stoic, Epictetus that the key is to focus on what is under our control not only connects with the minimalist attitude of getting rid of the superfluous while setting our own intentions but also maintains variety.

The Stoic Spirit of Plainness and Step-by-step Procedure Based upon the Self-belief got Though Minimalism has been widely praised in the recent past. Just as the Stoics declined to indulge wasteful, lavish habits, minimalists choose to leave aside pointless concerns and material consumption and to direct their attention to what really counts. This bond between ancient Stoicism and present minimalism carries us to find that these ideas are liked in the modern era, and they are source of great benefit in our lives. These principles apply also to the Cotode Stoics who find themselves in the quest for a simple life as a prescription for mental stability while the true essence of life is being left out of the rat race and using one's mind to compass spirit and a free spirit of a person indeed.

Although Stoicism virtually exemplifies the Western way of reasoning, the practice of minimalism is essentially as meaningful in the eastern way of reasoning. Jainism and Hinduism are some of the Eastern philosophies which are basically founded on the concept of Aparigraha which is in actuality a radical ideology of non-possessiveness and non-greed. The main idea hiding behind this theory is that individuals needing less material goods would become closer to the material world instead if they managed their materialistic desires.

Jainism believes, Aparigraha is the most significant confession made by the persona, except non-violence and truthfulness. They insist that the attachment to the material objects creates the feeling of greed and that leads to suffering from the necessity of competition and the resultant gill. The Jains believe that by the virtue of Aparigraha one can save himself from the desires of materialism and instead can get the redemption of spiritual life. This is actually the main thing that is lived by the Jain monks and nuns, who maintain simple, unadulterated lifestyles and living with nature harmoniously.

Moreover, Hinduism endorses Aparigraha to the extent of seeing it as a channel to spiritual and internal peace. According to Hinduism, the search for wealth and the accumulation of material possessions can be an obstruction to spiritual evolution. In addition to the removal of desire, individuals can, thus, focus not on the material aspect of life but on the connection with the Spiritual. This approach to simplicity and spiritual growth is perfectly consistent with the minimalism's principles. By the way, that's the way the minimalism community promotes minimalism concepts and becomes free from all distractions. This community of practice functions on the basis that human beings should be stripped of any extras or luxuries so that they are able to connect with their innermost beings.

Buddhism, like other Eastern philosophies extols the virtues of living the good life by being mindful with a bent toward minimalism. The Buddha taught that human suffering comes from their attachment to and ultimate suffering from desire. If we just cut off these bonds, then we can be in a tranquilized state, hence, propelling ourselves to Nirvä|na. Stress-free living is an issue that is addressed in Buddhism. It is a part of the concept of non-attachment and mindfulness and implies the ability to be purely here and now.

Buddhists, who are monks or nuns, refer to their Monastic life which represents their the simple life. Buddhists strictly follow the rules of conduct living monastic life. It is their own path to nirvana-rebirth, Buddhism, which restricts material distraction but fosters with the mindfulness, wisdom, and compassion of the people. This lifestyle that requires them to do away with distractions and be more focused on meditation that calls for more attention as they avoid thinking about the past or the future, and focus on the current moment.

Stoicism, Jainism, Hinduism, and Buddhism are the ancient philosophies that symbolize the idea of lasting happiness and contentment with life not through the accumulation of wealth and overt riches, but through a living style of intention, simplicity, and inner virtues. It is the same foundational minimalists that commented on the inner journey to a fulfilled and meaningful life, long before minimalism ever came.

Perhaps the best thing that can come from the dissemination of these ancient yet timeless lessons is the ability to shift the discussion so that we start making less of consumerism and material gain and more of meaningfulness. Additionally, the issues of facing the assumptions received in the modern world that the formula for living a good life is material wealth, and the imagination of simpler and better life are jobless.

The roots of minimalism run deep, extending far beyond the modern movement we see today. They are ingrained in the wisdom of ancient thinkers who realized that the good life is not realized by the store of wealth but by the neglect of inner virtues with a purposeful living. In our effort to deal with the challenges through the modern world, these ageless values of simplicity, being mindful, and creating an intentional life are the ways to a higher level of happiness, fulness, and tranquility.

Modern Interpretations

Minimalism, as a way of life, has always adhered to simplicity, gratification, and the willful reduction of life's supersedes. Minimalism can trace its origins to philosophies from centuries ago, but the two most recent centuries have shown a new kind of minimalism, which was really a comeback period where this lifestyle was now shaped by the problems of late modern society. As the world has gotten more and more complicated with so much more production and consumption of goods, the philosophy of minimalism has been transformed from a niche to a mainstream lifestyle. Today, minimalism is much more than just about the possession of fewer things. It is a comprehensive solution to personal well-being that helps more people to recover time, space, and mental cleanliness and thus offers a shelter from the ever-accelerating everyday life.

The upsurge of minimalism in the contemporary period has given a clear response to the ever-increasing consumer culture that dominated the 20th century. The establishment of mass production that followed the industrial revolution in turn resulted in unprecedented access to commodities. What used to be a privilege was now common and eventually, consumerism took over as the key component of the modern era. Adverts, media, and societal standards pointed to material wealth as the only path to success and happiness while also sending out a message that more is always better.

This is the setting for the rise of minimalism, which can be described as the advocacy for a simpler lifestyle as opposed to the patronage of material wealth and overconsumption, which has been the dominant paradigm before. The precursors of modern minimalism were those who were the first to reduce unimportant stuff and focus on what was the most significant to them. This movement became stronger as the cost of consumerism on the psychological and environmental sides was realized and at the same time, people desired greater autonomy.

In the last few years, minimalism became a global sensation with thought leaders such as Joshua Fields Millburn and Ryan Nichodemus, known collectively as The Minimalists, who played an important part in making it so. By their books, podcasts, and documentaries, The Minimalists have encouraged millions to re-evaluate their overassociation with material possessions through a more intentional approach to life. Their main point is that minimalism does not mean to live in a very deprived way, but it is about letting go of things and ideas that do not serve us so that we can give room to those that are worthwhile and meaningful. In other words, individuals can now prioritize their health, relationships, passions, and personal growth in their lives, which consequently lead them to be more contented and meaningful.

Additionally, Marie Kondo, a Japanese organizing consultant and author, has been one of the main figures in the minimum movement in the general public by her KonMari method of removing all the superfluous things from every corner of our homes. Kondo, a person who is attracted to the concept of the items we possess that "spark joy," she teaches about the time-tested practice of eliminating items that do not bring joy. As a result, countless people have been helped by Kondo to change the atmosphere in their homes, and thus have a positive impact on their lives. There is a simple, yet very important, message that is behind her thought: By creating our environment on purpose, we sincerely become affected by the surroundings and, thus, it becomes possible to create a balance which will get us nourished and supported.

Those modern interpretations of minimalism show a massive turn from a narrow view of just eliminating the clutter to building wellbeing at the same time. Today minimalism has become the answer to more than just a question, what are we acquiring? Living a life synonymous with our deepest values and priorities is a way of real minimalism as we see it as well as less materialistic. It is a state of mindfulness that goes beyond physical objects to include all spheres of life starting from time utilization to the way we handle technology.

Furthermore, intersection of minimalism with other contemporary movements remains a vivid indicator of its ability to adopt to the modern world and be relevant. The tiny house movement serves as an example of minimalism's influence on housing and living spaces. Advocates of tiny living are the ones who choose to reduce the sizes of their homes to the places normally less than a few hundred square feet, hence reducing the costs of their lives, shrinking their environmental impacts, and focusing on experiences á la- materially. This movement is a nice demonstration of minimalism living which can be used to create alternate more sustainable and intentional ways of living.

Just as the slow living movement, which tells people to take it slow and appreciate small happy moments of life, is ingrained with minimalist ideas as well. Slow living advocates for more intentional living, whereby one measures his/her personal success based on the improvement of their relationships with others and improvement of their inner self rather than the materialistic approach. Whether it's through cooking, travel, or daily routines, those who embrace slow living seek to cultivate a sense of mindfulness and contentment that is often lost in the hustle and bustle of modern life.

Digital minimalism, which is one other branch of the minimalist movement, solves the specific problems of the digital era. With technology on a hyperdrive, many people get constantly bombarded with the tip-tipping of notifications, emails, and social media updates. Digital minimalism is a way to regain command of your concentration and mental space using your wits to intentionally limit digital distractions. Through a reduction in the use of screens, the control of digital content, and rules for tech use, people can create more time for tasks that require deep thoughts, meaningful talks, and real life interactions.

What is so amazing in these contemporary versions of minimalism is the variety they have. Minimalism today can't be reduced to only one of the ways, but it is a very adaptable and personal reasoning that is designed for everybody's needs and conditions. Some people consider minimalism to be living in a small house or green lifestyle. Others think it is the reduction of materialism, slowing down, being present, or disconnecting from the digital world. But, whatever it is, all of these approaches involve a commitment to live with a purpose and to concentrate on what actually matters.

This diversity is really of great help to minimalism because it helps this philosophy to resonate with the minds of a great number of people, who are from different cultures and lead different lifestyles. Whether one gets attracted to minimalism due to the environmental benefits it brings, its capacity to lessen stress and unease, or the pledge to a larger freedom and control, the core messages are still the same: simplicity, focus, and the core.

In some ways, contemporary minimalist movement could be perceived as a continuation of those ancient philosophical traditions which have for long time supported the idea of simplicity and intentional living. Although the context may look different, the essential human aspiration to have a life full of meaning, clarity, and happiness remains unvaried. Through modern minimalism that offers a new interpretation of these basic ideas which everyone knows, one can find his/her way in a complex and uncertain present.

We tend to find it quite a struggle to deal with customer culture, overconsumption of technology, and the speed of life, by minimalism we find a way to happ..., providing a path to greater freedom, happiness, and mental peace. It is an invitation for us to take another look at our beliefs about what living a good life really is, and to try planning that it might be that, less is more. Minimalism comes in many forms and the style of minimal architecture is extremely good for that purpose and it still a simple landmark for the sustainable development, which permanently underlines that the main treasures of life are actually the most elementary ones.

Minimalism vs. Consumerism

The 20th-century experience was a highly life-changing one for human societies in terms of reaping good things like wealth, success, and happiness. The use of large-scale production methods and marketing initiatives and the widespread availability of consumer goods make it that the new cultural model developed: consumerism. This process leads to a complete change in the way people live, thereby reshaping their desires, values, and lifestyles. In essence, consumerism is made on the idea that joy and satisfaction can be found in possessing materials. The overrunning the world the arrival of this belief brought at it turned out too apparent was the fact that the pursuit of more did not bring relief but became the reason for people to grapple with a lack of fulfillment, confusion, and dissatisfaction. Unlike the existing order, minimalism suggests a different route learning to enjoy your life through the use of few products that bring you maximum pleasure and well-being.

At its onset, the growth of the consumerism culture was funded by the industrial revolution that witnessed the emergence of unprecedented levels of production and consumption. Largely due to the introduction of new manufacturing technologies, goods discontinued of the past become omnipresent and low-cost ones. This development was marked by the speeding up of a nascent advertising industry which was of great import for molding consumer behaviour. Advertisers initiated the concept that goods sold happiness, success, and social status if bought - therefore, people started to acquire such goods starting with the everyday household appliances and moving on to various luxury goods. Consequently, the enjoyment of materialistic possessions was equated with real happiness and thus quickly consumerism established itself as the main characteristic of the modern world.

The consumerist thinking is based on the idea of endless longings. Advertisements and marketing are designed to manipulate people into thinking that they are in need of one thing or another and therefore they have to spend a lot of money in order to get these things. This intensified demand for commodities that are of the latest models and possess the most recent concepts inadvertently forms a rampant culture of consumerism. It becomes habitual firm therefore increasingly hard to break through increased production and aurora of new commodities. That "more buys more funnies" concept is fascinating but not often the case in fact more will only lead to overcrowded disorder in their lives as both the psyche and the physical environment get fuller with some objects that offer satisfaction but not real joy.

Consumerism has far-reaching impacts, not only on individuals but also on the environment. The craving for more and more goods implies a higher production of these, which in its turn necessitates a lot of resource extraction, energy consumption and waste. The high ecological cost of consumer culture has been well documented, with the problems of pollution, deforestation and climate change directly related to over-consumption. In this context, the goal of getting more is neither feasible nor is it advisable given the fact that it is endangering the planet and humanity in general.

Minimalism is a counter movement that has emerged due to the excesses of consumerism, and it has come up as a strong force for changing the existing perspective. By its nature, the concept of minimalism bravely fights the idea of happiness and fulfillment in outward elements. In its place, it suggests that people should cherish good relationships, life experiences, self-development and health to be happy. By promoting quality as a superior alternative to everything no matter how much of it is or is not, the minimalists aim at living on purpose to genuinely understand life rather than become baffled by the things.

One of the mantras of minimalism is the idea that less is more. This idea is not about self-depriving of the things that bring joy, rather it is about making a choice with the mindful awareness of the intended effect of the purchase. Minimalists are those individuals only who possess the items that add value to their lives; and they are ready for everything to go in return. This process of de-accumulation is not just about clearing physical space, but also about freeing the mind from the distractions and anxieties that come with excess. Minimalists thus are given freedom in their lives to do what they love, connect with people, and develop themselves as human beings through the process of simplifying their lives.

The psychological effect of consumerism can be greatly significant. Living in a cluttered, materialist society can often cause stress, anxiety, and an ostensible dissatisfaction. The never-ending messages about buying and the pressure to stick to what society expects can make one feel powerless and unfulfilled. With minimalism, one can learn to let go of those things, to be honest with oneself and to make decisions that would bring them real pleasure and comfort. By rejecting the pursuit of more, people who live a minimalist life often get hold of a feeling of peace and being happy which was previously unavailable.

Another advantage of minimalism other than its mental benefits is the reduced strain it puts on the environment. Through less demand, minimalists lead to sustainability in various ways of living. The practice of being a minimalist includes the idea of conscious consumption which in turn becomes less. The following of this practice not only depletes the environmental impact of one's lifestyle but also strengthens the appreciation for the resources and the products used. The term Minimalism, in this respect, is not just a personal choice but a step taken towards sustainability and preservation in the broader context of saving the planet for upcoming generations.

Even though, the consumer attitude promotes the view that one\'s getting of goods brings him more happiness, minimalism, on the other hand, says that life is complete by reducing the number of possessions to those that have value and by making certain of the clarity and purpose of the way people live. They are aware that the actual satisfaction that is never achievable through gaining more objects comes from the people and things one is passionate about, that is, the acquisition of skills, socializing with likeminded people, and experiencing simple pleasures. By relinquishing the incessant craving for more, minimalists not only lead cluttered lives but also realize who they are and live in sync with their principles.

Minimalism versus consumerism is a very severe battle. Consumerism drives people to continually retrieve the goods and products that eventually pile up, deface the environment and make them feel so bitter by endless nagging thoughts of things that aren\'t available. Minimalism, however, takes into account the notion that high quality is better than quantity and the concept that actual fulfillment arises from immaterial stuff. The psychological burden brought about by consumerism is quite severe on some people, but minimalism is a way of getting an escape route from the pressures and living a rather meaningful and contented life. The positive effects on the environment of going minimal further establish its importance in dealing with the overreaching by consumerism and in showing how less consumption can lead to a more sustainable lifestyle that protects the earth\'s resources.

Although the whole world is trying to deworm itself from the overconsumption of resources, minimalism remains a very strong and relevant belief that will give the people concerned the basis for a worthier and more contented life. By questioning the precepts of consumer culture and advocating for a simpler and more conscientious lifestyle, minimalism is a way to a happier and quieter life, also to a. It may serve as a device to tell us that the essentials can be bartered but the pursuit of excess is oftentimes a hindrance to the joys and fulfillment which are at times inaccessible through other means.

Living with Purpose

In a world increasingly characterised by speed, excess, and the relentless pursuit of more, the concept of living with purpose offers a refreshing and profoundly transformative alternative. Living with purpose is about aligning one's life with core values and priorities, making intentional choices about how to spend time, energy, and resources. It is a practice that invites us to strip away the superfluous and focus on what truly matters, allowing for a more meaningful and fulfilling existence. Minimalism, as a philosophy and lifestyle, provides a powerful framework for living with purpose, helping individuals to identify their true priorities and eliminate the distractions that often obscure them.

Intentional living lies at the heart of this approach. It involves making conscious decisions about how we allocate our resources—be they time, energy, or material possessions—so that they align with our deepest values and aspirations. In contrast to a life lived on autopilot, where choices are often driven by external pressures or societal expectations, intentional living requires us to pause, reflect, and make deliberate decisions that reflect our true selves. It is an ongoing process of self-awareness and mindfulness, where each action is guided by a clear sense of purpose.

Minimalism is intrinsically linked to intentional living. At its core, minimalism encourages us to identify what is truly important to us and to let go of anything that distracts from these priorities. This process begins with the physical—decluttering our homes and living spaces—but extends far beyond material possessions. It involves evaluating every aspect of our lives, including our commitments, relationships, and even our thoughts, to determine whether they contribute to or detract from a purposeful life. In this way, minimalism serves as a tool for cutting through the noise and focusing on what really matters.

One of the most profound benefits of living with purpose through minimalism is the clarity it brings. In a world filled with distractions, it is easy to lose sight of our goals and values, becoming entangled in activities and pursuits that do not truly serve us. Minimalism offers a way to reclaim our focus, allowing us to see clearly what is essential and what is not. This clarity extends to every area of life, from the physical spaces we inhabit to the mental and emotional landscapes we navigate. By simplifying our environment and eliminating unnecessary distractions, we create the space needed to concentrate on our true priorities.

For example, someone who values creativity might find that a cluttered environment stifles their ability to think freely and express themselves. By embracing minimalism, they can simplify their surroundings, reducing distractions and creating a space that fosters inspiration and creative flow. This could mean having a clean, organised workspace, free from unnecessary items, or limiting the number of projects they take on at any given time to focus deeply on one creative endeavour. In this way, minimalism supports their purpose by providing the conditions necessary for their creativity to flourish.

Similarly, someone who values family might find that their time is consumed by work commitments or social obligations that leave little room for meaningful connections with loved ones. By applying the principles of minimalism to their schedule, they can identify which activities truly contribute to their well-being and happiness and eliminate those that do not. This might involve reducing work hours, saying no to non-essential commitments, or simplifying daily routines to spend more quality time with family. Through minimalism, they can align their daily actions with their value of family, creating a life that is richer in connection and love.

Living with purpose through minimalism also brings a profound sense of satisfaction. When our actions are in alignment with our values, we experience a deep sense of fulfilment that goes beyond the fleeting pleasures of material possessions or superficial achievements. This satisfaction comes from knowing that we are living authentically, that our choices reflect who we truly are, and that we are making progress towards our long-term goals. It is a sense of contentment that is rooted in purpose and intentionality, rather than in external validation or societal expectations.

Minimalism challenges the notion that fulfilment can be found in the accumulation of more—more possessions, more achievements, more status. Instead, it invites us to consider the possibility that true fulfilment comes from needing less, from focusing on what is truly essential and letting go of the rest. This shift in perspective is both liberating and empowering, as it allows us to take control of our lives and make choices that are aligned with our deepest values and desires.

The process of aligning our lives with our values through minimalism is not always easy. It requires us to confront difficult truths about what we truly want and to make sometimes challenging decisions about what to let go of. However, the rewards are immense. By living with purpose, we create a life that is not only simpler and less cluttered but also more meaningful, fulfilling, and aligned with our true selves.

As you reflect on your own life, consider how minimalism might help you to live with greater purpose. What are your core values? What truly matters to you? And how might you simplify your life to focus more on these priorities? By embracing minimalism as a tool for intentional living, you can create a life that is not only more aligned with your values but also more fulfilling and joyful.

Minimalism is not about restrictions or limitations. It is about creating the freedom to live a life that is true to who you are. By letting go of the excess and focusing on what truly matters, you can align your daily actions with your long-term goals and values, creating a life that is rich in purpose and meaning. This is the true essence of minimalism—living with intention, clarity, and a deep sense of purpose.

Chapter 2
The Psychological Benefits of Minimalism

Indeed, the hyperactive rhythm of existence with the help of modern technologies and daily hurly-burly that brings the necessity to think and memory can also provoke a person to become injured. The obligations of our daily life—be it the multitude of things one should do and the infinite ways of doing them, the constant need to remain online, or the overwhelming avalanche of both physical and mental supplies—may give rise to excessive stress, anxiety and a declining sense of well-being. It is the frame within which the minimalist trend becomes evident as not only a matter of lifestyle but as the best remedy for the current mental burden of the civilization. Minimalism paves the way for responding to the mental blockades of the hurried Western civilization by introducing a method of mental decluttering. It does this by promoting the intentional simplification of our lives which, in turn, ensures that we obtain mental clarity and emotional steadiness and contentment at a higher level.

Minimalism, as a practice of inclusion-exclusion, is a way of cutting off the irrelevant, the superfluous and the distracting thus holding attention to the essentials. Although this concept of minimalism can be practiced in different areas of life, its power in psychological health is most remarkable. A time where we reduce the number of decisions we ought to make each day, for example, minimalism decreases the mental fatigue that is usually associated with too many options. Decision fatigue is a passable idea of the human mind, the tiredness, and the ability to make decisions when there are a large number of them to process it. Imagine a situation wherein we have countless options before us, decision fatigue if not mentioned, could be the norm apart from postponed decision-making and the general notion of chaos. The program becomes proactive in cutting down options on the basis of its inclination; hence, it aids to preserve our psychological energy for truly deserving decisions, thereby endorsing clear and effective thinking.

Moreover, the concept of minimalism directly deals with the stress that results from living in cluttered, chaotic environments. It is a fact, that clutter has a direct psychological impact on us because it produces negative states of worry, also makes us unable to focus and a furthermore brings sensation of guilt. Moreover, the mere act of tidying up - that is taking away such items that are not having any useful purpose - has a very strong positive effect on feelings of stress we have. A minimalist environment that has things in order, is uncomplicated, and has free space is conducive to a state of serenity and mastery which is often missing in more cluttered environments. As you organize your physical space, you will naturally organize your mental space as well. A tidier area can also help lead to a clearer mind, especially with the removal of visual and mental noise that occurs when there is clutter.

Furthermore, apart from the alleviation of stress, minimalism also acts as an enabler in increasing our mental capacity and concentration. Today, the sky is the limit in terms of the digital age, and the clutter of information, stimuli, and distractions has, in turn, made focusing even harder. The minimalist approach, which focuses on the elimination of the unnecessary, provides a tactic to face up to this dilemma. Through selective filtering of the contents of our environments and digital spaces of what is generally irrelevant and unnecessary, we set the right conditions for concentrating, and sustaining concentration of attention. Certainly, this becomes crucial in an era where multitasking is often praised, and seems to be the 'in' thing, despite its known biomechanical ramifications that the recent literature has evidenced. Beliefs accused of technology-induced laziness are combated by Minimalists whose approach is about the refraining of busy thoughts and focusing to awaken creativity and mental agility.

It is not only the reduction of stress and the enhancement of wealth that minimalism carries with it. It provides much of the emotional development of a human being as well. Happiness and the acquisition of material things are most often linked together in a society where voracious shopping is taken as a norm. Nevertheless, this search brings about disillusionment more often than not. Americans generally have a higher standard of living compared to people in the rest of the world. Yet, their happiness index exerts little influence on the rest of the world. The realization of the caducity of life and material wealth is like a wake-up call that will change the way people perceive life and their selves. After the acquisition, the new products soon become boring and thus needless and empty space is left to fill. Minimalism solves our leading anxiety by a radical focus shift, from the accumulation of goods to an inner peace driven by less.

Another reason for the existence of psychology students is that they learn how to communicate better with others. Then they are more likely to achieve success in other areas too. One of the five factors included in psychology students' help is the communication one. It is really impressive what the effects of learning the skills of psychology and communication studies are and I am sure that it is essential to teach them to everyone irrespective of their major. Students with ideas how to use communication effectively with other students evoke discussion that fosters new ways of solving problems and thinking about potential issues etc. Moreover, the teachers would have the opportunity to react and correct the position of the students which would lead to the discovery of the truth. Apart from that, they must be advocates of the LGBTQI and women who disagree with the physical grooming that society inflicts on them and who debate the importance of much-needed counsel and cranial energy to heal oneself. Minimalism can be a tool for individuals so that they can construct their world in the way they desire it to be. Hence, even though a limited number of students attain basics skills in communication, it is important that more should be involved in the attempt.

It is interesting to note that foods that are labeled and sold as superfoods are not always green. Some are already locally grown and are not high in the price, this actually becomes an advantage. The vertical gardens which can be powered by syringes may have five plants for each of the four branches of the syringes. Vitamin K, Folic acid, fiber, and other nutrients of this kind are mainly found in the environment. Therefore, it is better to let farms grow naturally rather than depending on the required inputs from modern society which on the other hand, is a threat to the environment. The main reason why this issue is in existence makes people understand that additives and pesticides used in this era in agricultural production pose a threat to the environment.

Another way minimalism collaborates with human existence is it gives one individual freedom and a sense of the power to decide and control their course of life. Even in the times when workers are almost entirely replaced by the dominance of machines, the people who are still able to adapt and live a life that matters feel more fulfilled than those whose lives seem too empty in the crowded world of objects and low-value businesses. For instance, people, especially the elderly are less prone to follow their ambitions, which in the past were the cause of their realization. Some say that the limited number of the jobs are responsible for this. Consumers and business executives are the main

Additionally, minimalism breeds emotional resilience that is more and more crucial nowadays. When we loosen our attachment to the material world and the admiration and acceptance of others, we are less prone to become confident through the inevitable fluctuations of life. It doesn't matter whether we talk about a loss of a job, a change in circumstances, or the aging process, minimalism is the key to the recovery of inner power that comes from expecting enough and keeping life's balance. By relying on this resilience, we can sail through the highs and lows in life with more poise, aware that our happiness is not dictated by external factors but is instead connected to our deep sense of purpose and intentionality.

As we uncover the mental health rewards of minimalism, it is apparent that it goes beyond merely helping us tidy our homes or declutter our stuff. It is a potent instrument that aids the operation of our brain, the reduction of our load and the promotion of emotional health. By incorporating minimalism, we not only simplify our outer lives but also develop a more focused, and therefore, a more fulfilling inner life. This way, we pave the way for real happiness that does not come and go like a mirage or is conditioned by external circumstances, but that comes from a clear mind, a peaceful soul and a purposeful life.

Reducing Decision Fatigue

In the world of up-to-minute life, the multitude of options we face each day can be overwhelming. As the sun rises, choices present themselves to us: whether to put on our clothes, to eat, to spend time, or even to communicate with the people around us. Although the freedom to choose is often identified as a quintessential expression of personal elegance, such vast sets of opportunities may cause what is called decision fatigue. Decision fatigue is a case where the mental energy needed for different decisions in a day is overused, which results in worse choices, lower willpower, and a feeling of mental tiredness. In a world where alternatives appear to be endless, minimalism is an excellent solution to this evolutional disease by promoting the straightforwardness of our lives and the deliberate exclusion of unnecessary choices.

The notion of decision fatigue was initially introduced by the psychologists who noticed that people usually tend to make less and less judicious decisions after having to take a series of decisions. This is due to the cognitive resources required for decision-making being limited, whereas as their depletion, our capacity to think clearly and make rational judgments decrease. In our daily lives, it can cause as ill-considered purchases, procrastination, or simply the feeling of being overwhelmed that decreases our productivity and our overall well-being.

Minimalism, being simple and aimed at tuning, provides the effective antidote to the problem of decision fatigue, which is by simplifying the decision-making process. Reduction in the number of choices to be made by adapting a minimum style will cause us to retain our cognitive faculties for more demanding tasks. One of the most practical examples of this is the capsule wardrobe. A capsule wardrobe is composed of several items that are interchangeable and that you can make many outfits with. Now, instead of navigating through a crammed closet every day and figuring out what can go with this, people can clear their minds of these thoughts and use the mental space to concentrate on more paramount activities. Such an approach is not only effective in terms of decisions but also encourages mental clarity and ease.

The advantages of the clearing of decision fatigue through minimalism go further than the area of clothing. The question then arises: What kind of meal should I prepare how to organize my schedule and do I have to change anything to get space to move? These and many other questions you can shape very practically by applying minimal ideas in every direction. For instance, the weekly plan allows for a limited number of meals to be made, by which people will be able to relieve mental pressure from choosing what to cook. Then, by introducing a prepared calendar that would restrict us to core tasks, our time management would be more efficient and our cognitive load less experienced. We could also, by living in the order and proper storing of our things to places which are easily reached also get used to the idea that we do not have to think where to find items and only use the content for productive purposes.

Studies confirm that reducing the amount of choices faced by an individual brings about a higher level of satisfaction and better cognitive performance. A study by psychologists Sheena Iyengar and Mark Lepper has been described in the past as proof of a thesis. It is filled with the fact that the consumers who have a broader array of choices initially lure the clients, but the latter are more willing to purchase and are more satisfied when facing a limited selection to choose from. This is the focal point of the paradox of choice, where the too-many-alternatives devastatingly lead to the waste of time and despair. The other side of the matter is the positive job of minimalism in terms of the psychological health of the human being. By taking the initiative and cutting down on the number of options readily available, we can make ourselves more immune to the debilitating effects of decision fatigue and thereby be in charge of our lives and happy.

The philosophy of minimalism strengthens the idea that we should pay attention to quality, rather than the quantity of material goods. If we, for example, owning a few but a majority of high-quality things is a start to the process of reining in the numerous acquisition, maintenance, and usage decisions would be impacted by this and we, in turn, would need far less time and energy to make these decisions. However, to be short and to the point; this transition is also noticeable in every aspect of our life including our relationship, work, and leisure activities. Something to do with it is doing things that matter and setting ourselves on the right track, which can be done by omitting the superfluous and molt unique entities that frequently come with a multitude of alternatives.

In addition to the physical cleanliness that minimalism brings, it also has a substantial effect on decision fatigue and a person's mental health. The constant need to make choices in the digital age might be responsible for stress, anxiety, and the feeling of defeat. Minimalism, in return, offers a gateway for improving the situation, by forming a structured approach to daily living. Its main goal is to reduce the information that surrounds us and that comes from our daily routine. Hence, a clear and consistent environment does much to fuel the mental calm and fortitude needed to face life's many challenges correctly. This, counterfeit, grants us the possibility to assume we will make better decisions not influenced by exterior factors because our values and goals have been properly embraced.

The phenomenon of decision fatigue in minimizing practices is possibly the most eloquently showcased in the realm of digital consumption. In a world where we receive emails, notifications, and other kinds of informational spoils, we are often faced with decision-making dilemmas. Technological minimalism is a modification of the minimalistic concept and implies a deliberate selection of our digital environments. Intentional actions like not surfing the net, caution when signing up for any notice which is not important, and on top of all that being picky on your media consumption, are all practical measures in reducing decision fatigue. Professional expertise is great for the economy. Even quality is connected with the culture and peace in the country.

Largely, minimalism is a strategy of not just holding on to only essential inside commodities only but rather it is definitely about making a few, important decisions. By focusing on the decline of choices we face every day we can save our mental energy for the decisions that matter, which then will lead to greater clarity, satisfaction, and well-being. The slimming of minimalism is one of the most popular ways to cure the tiredness of decision that is the characteristic of modern living. This basically means that you get to live life with more purpose, focus, and overall satisfaction.

The minimalist form of choosing in life that will not only us survive the complexities of our modern living but will also give us a breathing space from the excessive number of first-person questions in our immediate surroundings. With the help of simplicity and intentionality, we can relieve ourselves from the cognitive stress of decision fatigue and live a life that is not only easier but also a life that has a deeper meaning and a greater joy in it. In an environment in which the prevailing attitude is usually more for the same, less is more is especially apparent when the decisions we make lead to our lives.

Stress Reduction

As part of our busy modern lives, stress has become a common factor we all reckon with, not sparing any of our daily routines, our minds, and even our homes. We can often feel besieged and drained by the continual demands of our work, social life, and information technology, as we become earthbound in its infinite complexity. While the stress response is a nature-born reaction to the challenges of life, however, when the body is continuously exposed to stressors in an environment with so much clutter and excess, this can have a disastrous effect on our mental and physical health. It is against this bad backdrop that minimalism rises as a key strategy for stress reduction, a means of achieving a more relaxed, well-balanced life.

One of the major factors causing stress is a clutter-free, both for mental and physical issues. A cluttered environment, such as a crowded house with lots of unnecessary items or a packed-out schedule, is a significant source of disorder and an uncontrollable situation. These distortions of order not only offset the ability to work but also create a detached mental background of anxiety. The many words and phrases teem with the existence of objects among us,' be they possessions, commitments, or even cognitive functions, crying for our undivided attention and energy, while we can hardly cope with even one while leaving out many others, are actually squeezing out of our little energy reserve the last droplets of oxygen.

Minimalism is the answer to this problem. It is a philosophy of carefully taking things away that are not necessary, so they don't bother us anymore.

De-cluttering—the process of liberating yourself from things you no longer use and giving them to people who need them—is not merely putting objects in boxes; it is a way of making a space that supports our well-being rather than destructs it. By clearing out spaces that are burdened with too many possessions, we bring some order, structure, and transparency that is known to be very pacifying. A minimalist home, which has clean surfaces and open spaces, gives me a feeling of peace and secrecy, helping me manage everything easily and keeping the resources intact and in a very clear manner throughout the day.

A mental state that is less cluttered is also associated with a lower quantity of physical clutter. They both induce the same set of stressors; thus, if a room is disorganised, the mind is likely disorganised too. During a part of the daily routine, our minds can become overloaded with the pressures of a busy schedule, others' expectations, and an avalanche of digital information. Minimalism calls for a simplification of physical and emotional things, thus being an aid in the necessity of a simple life. Through enabling and facilitating the solidisation of key cris, the removing of non-essentials, thus allowing the surrounding world to be part of the thinking process, an individual can invalidate outside disturbances. For example, it might mean setting limits on my work time, going out fewer times than usual, or giving myself a break from my phone. These elements cater to the space that allows me to ponder, release, and reflect on what happened in peace.

Financial difficulties are a vital cause of contemporary pressures. The obligation to achieve community-accepted symbols of being alert, self-reliant, successful, and wealthy results in unnecessary purchases, loan dependencies, and a circle of financial apprehension. Unlike the mentality, this consumer-focused way of operating is different when minimalism leads us. Through the clear, straightforward choice of goods and services instead of the overrated items proposed by marketers, where prices are much lower, we will achieve a huge percentage of financial benefits. This not only takes away the stress of financial difficulties but also one will have the ability to appreciate the available things more, the one bringing contentment and feeling of safety to him/herself.

A life of a minimalist, therefore, is a life with less time and energy spent on maintaining treasures and handling numerous jobs. Simply put, more items in our possession lead to less time which is used to clean, repair, or tidy them. Similarly, the more we try to manage more obligations, the less time and energy we will have. Minimalism is suggesting to remove nothing from both the material and spiritual resources we intend to use allowing only significant factors to be reached. Moreover, this is how we can get back precious mental energy and time that can be used in healthy and rewarding activities rather than in tiresome ones. Thus, the reliving of life through simplification and the victory of a healthy lifestyle over pressure are the keys to less distress and more well-being.

Furthermore, the minimalist philosophy promotes the state of mind of sufficiency instead of the lack model. In a time where the consumerist mentality that more is better is on the rise, minimalism reminds us that we can derive pleasure from little. Changing the way we think can change our stress levels. When we concentrate on the sufficiency of our lives—having enough rather than excessive tallying of our possessions—we take off the pressure of incessantly amassing unnecessary stuff. This wisdom could be applied throughout the future path we take. We would feel more secure and much less apprehensive rather than ungrateful regarding material property, as we fully understand the things we possess are not determinants of our happiness, rather the relationships we have with people are the ones.

Minimalism denotes the notion of being focused on the present moment rather than waiting for the future or remembering the past as being the place to find the solutions and happiness they seek in life, and it is one of those other things that are responsible for relieving the stress associated with its adoption. Nowadays, few of us can afford the luxury of a single goal pursuit at work and enjoy our lives in balance. They help us to hone our concentration and efficiency skills. It can happen in many ways, such as a simple meal without the company of the phone, family time, or thinking things through instead of jumping the gun. This is something that minimalism teaches us to deepen our connections and experiences. Our conscious focus on the present moment not only enables us a sense of fulfillment but also can deliver us from the fear of the future and the hurt from the past.

A growing body of evidence is giving its endorsement to the psychological merits of minimalism, especially the one relating to stress relief. A study has found that those who practice minimalism report lower incidences of anxiety in their lives, feel more competent and self-sufficient, and are generally more satisfied with their lives. This is not odd when we consider that minimalism is the match where our true character and values meet life's settings and the priorities we choose. Our love for the things we possess shows indirectly our real identity. The effects of such an alignment in behavior are thus, automatic and irreversible so it goes that the reduction of the dissonance between beliefs and behavior, or personal and collective needs can diminish the state of stress.

Hence reducing stress through minimalism is a militant methodology in this chaotic, demanding world. We create an environment that allows for the peace of mind and the clarity of thought necessary for our well-being, by eliminating everything that is unneeded in our lives or any form of disruption that is not beneficial including mental, physical, and financial ones. Minimalism allows us to focus on what is important, to live intentionally and simply, and to be content with what we have rather than what we do not. Thus, as we face the rigors of modernity, minimalism emerges as a very promising means to achieve tranquillity and happiness, offering us an avenue to handle life differently and consequently enjoy a more relaxed and joyful existence.

Mental Clarity and Focus

In today's rapidly evolving phase of life, where our lives are surrounded by multiple pivots and other people, and where those dealing with us are other than us, with clarity and continuity of thought and action and general new activities, the issue is very sensitive. We complain all the time that we do not have peace of mind and we cannot concentrate. We have a fragment of loads on our minds even though the world is currently disconnected from the internet. Mental turbulence in modern society is a consequence of physical chaos, similar to the physical clutter we can all put ourselves through. However, the solution is less the evolution of technology but more the strategy you decide to adopt. Minimalism, which leaves a narrow road, simplicity, and attention create a principle of the orderliness of thought that are capable of helping us overcome these obstacles and of course that of creativity. By way of its attribute, the reduction in both physical and mental clutter, minimalism, in other words, better focus and making decisions will be the direct result of the mental awakening and creative problem-solving that come from turning the storms of life into the peace of mind and the action of this coaching program in life.

The connection between physical clutter and mental clarity is intuitive and well-documented. When our surroundings are overflowing with unnecessary items, we can become visually and psychologically distracted, which makes concentrating on our important tasks almost impossible. The brain is configured to detect and comprehend the environment first and then to follow and understand where it will hence the time. Therefore, One turns to find the way and the way out of excess mental sorting and ordering in the physical world. This is also the reason why when one walks into a separate area that is cluttered one often feels stress and uneasiness in a room; the mind works on the excess visual information for instance the brain that does the work and simultaneously it becomes tired.

Minimalism solves the issue by calling on us to clean our places and offices of non-essential items. On the other hand, the way of making the area tidy is not the simple order, but we are to make the complex area where we can think ahead the order. The basic idea of a minimalist environment, which is free of anything unnecessary, allows people to relax and focus on the thing without allowing their minds to wander aimlessly on several different issues simultaneously. The focus is only on such a thing instead of the environment created which is not simple and directed to a function. Such an environment in the simplicity of everything creates a feeling of calm and order, confidence, and ease of thinking are the results. Thus, a person can easily make decisions.

A minimalist lifestyle can benefit one's productivity levels as well. When the distractions we face are cut down, the brain can immerse itself deeply in an assignment such that focus and efficiency improve. In today's work culture that frequently encourages multitasking despite it being proven to reduce overall productivity is even more critical for the success of any work. A minimalist workspace consisting of only the essential tools and materials allows an individual to focus on one task at a time, an ability that enhances both the quality and speed of their work. There is no need to look for tools or organize disheveled places thereby eliminating time wasti, and thus productivity is further facilitated.

Moreover, the minimalism principles can be applied not only to our physical but also to our virtual world as well. The world continues to bombard us with information which easily overwhelms us, resulting in a disorganized digital life. Firstly, a paper-filled email inbox which no one opened, the uninformed people posting endlessly on social media, the reminder bell that does not cease to ring are all contributing to creating cognitive overload. Pillars of this digital clutter, in addition to creating situations in which we fail, also fragment our motion and attention span. We cannot balance both the primary task and the ultimate objective.

Digital minimalism is an approach that has recently been gaining popularity as a solution to this contemporary problem. By controlling one's online footprint and thoughtfully regulating information flows, digital minimalism is proven effective in minimizing the need to be constantly hooked to the web. This may take the form of unsubscribing from unnecessary email lists, creating limits for social media use, or applying tools that prevent one from being distracted by non-essential sites during work hours. The aim is to have a digital climate that, like the minimalist space, is strategically planned and completely free of unnecessary distractions, providing a chance for the mind to focus entirely on what is really acclaimed as important without being perpetually disturbed by digital technological advancement.

The impact of reducing both physical and digital clutter on mental clarity and focus cannot be overstated. The mind's processing of irrelevant stimuli is lessened, hence the heightened capability to think about the most important things. Logical reasoning and creative thinking are boosted as the brain can gear its attention toward solving problems. Uninterrupted deep work is rare in today's world full of distractions but is crucial for any progress made in life. By restricting the unnecessary, minimalism sets the stage for sometimes even deep work, a state that is essential for success in any given area.

Furthermore, the mental clarity that comes from a minimalist lifestyle also enhances creativity. There are times when the creative process requires a little freedom of the mind—thus allowing new ideas to arrive, merge, and reenact the stage. When the brain is in disarray due to excessive information or too many tasks, creative thinking can hardly break through such clutters. Through the simplification of the environment and routine, minimalism prepares the setting that gives birth to creativity. Artists, writers, and other professionals of the creative world have thus adopted minimalism as a means of realizing their artistic potential. The mental sharpness and concentration that minimalism offers let one easily spot similarities between things, and relate them, leading to the invention of fresh ideas, all of which are essential to the act of creation.

Having said that, the mental discipline of minimalism makes a very important contribution to mental clarity too, by putting a big emphasis on intentionality. Minimalism gives the individual a chance to take a conscious effort on the matters, they, would want to allow in their life—from possessions, to information, or commitments. This intentionality extends to how we spend our time and energy, ensuring that our actions align with our values and goals. By opting for better ways to use our brains that do not involve the mental fatigue that oversubscription or pointless activities generate we can keep our minds clear. Such an attitude not only destroys the causes of stress but also boosts our ability to focus on things truly important.

Simply put, minimalism is a highly effective strategy for gaining mental lucidity and concentration in an environment that does tend to be overwhelming. One can create not only the physical environment but also the digital workspace that fosters creative ways of thinking, thus, it is helpful to declutter yourself, both the soul, and the mind. This can lead to more in-depth involvement in one's work, the discovery of more efficient solutions to problems, and ultimately drawing from one's creative capacities. The distinctive aspect, which is also the attributive reason of minimalism is the instrument for sharpening and focusing the mind, thereby making it possible to manage the intricacies of contemporary living with style and efficiency.

Minimalism principles can be a reference point for all of us as we continue to deal with the demands of an information-packed and speedy society. Through accepting non-complex options and living a very conscious way of each moment in our life either in the mental or emotional context, we can "see" the needed space for creation of a working environment or the broadening of personal horizons. By doing the above, apart from being more productive and innovative, one would also have a feeling of satisfaction and opportune goal setting in life.

Emotional Well-Being

We live in a world of prodigality where accumulation of material goods is a symbol of success and happiness and thus, we tend to ignore the benefits of minimalism. However, minimalism, a philosophical approach that involves embracing simplicity and mindful consumption displays a trustworthy argument that having less can enhance our emotional well-being. Minimalism is the contrary of deprivation as it is an invitation to bring to the fore those things in life that we genuinely love, those that fulfill us, and the ones that guarantee happiness over time. This change in viewpoint is able to both engender greater happiness and also boost our appreciation of the aspects of life that are not material which are definitely a much more reliable source of emotional well-being.

Among the most meaningful ways that minimalism affects emotional health is by stimulating individuals to appreciate first what is truly important. In a society driven by consumption, we receive infinite signals that tell us the value of a person is determined by the amount of money, status, or possessions they have. Nevertheless, both studies and our personal experiences tell us that the more we own our possessions, the shorter the beauty of them will be. Instead of purchasing and operating anything, we waste a lot of time and energy in the acquisition cycle which results in our emotional injuries due to dissatisfaction. This vicious cycle that involves obtaining and being unhappy may be detrimental to our emotional health which leads to unfulfilled life and material wealth.

Minimalism provides the answer to this cycle by changing the focus from what we lack to what we possess. Minimalism makes it possible for individuals to be authentic rather than through material goods by seeing beyond the products and blemishes and recognizing the true depth of their lives and these are our relationships, experiences, and personal growth. Many surveys actually indicate that these are the areas most closely linked to genuine happiness over many years. We create a life that prioritizes these elements of happiness besides material acquisitions, which is not only simple but also rich and real, and thus joyful.

Living with less developing a higher understanding of the present moment and of the resources we usually take for granted. Once the impetuous need for more is gone, we can be aware and grateful for the beauty of ordinary things like the smile of a close one, the soul-calming stillness of nature, and the satisfaction of doing a job right really bring happiness to us at the moment. This attitude which is a result of adopting a minimalistic way of life can help us foster our emotional health as it allows us to live in the now and sense life deeply. We often reach the highest levels of the flow of component and happiness in those uncomplicated moments devoid of superfluous distractions.

Moreover, minimalism addresses the cycle of consumerism which can provide short-term pleasure but long-term dissatisfaction problems and provides the solution to them. The marketing strategy is that happiness can be bought and the next thing you buy will be the moment of finally being really satisfied. This process might not be the right thing; the new things might bring us a short-lived sense of peace, and then we will be almost automatically looking for the next item to fill the gap. This action that causes ultimate satisfaction and happiness by taking everything that we have and being happy with its simplicity is suggested by minimalism.

A critical change in orientation from acquisition to appreciation can remarkably affect our emotional resilience. In the absence of striving for the possession of material goods and the comparison with others, envy, or inadequacy shall not rule our state of being. In place of that, instead of feeling the lack of necessities and the situation be grateful for, a feeling of abundance and a sense of gratitude prevail, which consequently results in a more temperate view of the world. This sort of emotional strength is very important to deal with the ups and downs of life since it enables us to be cool and happy despite the unfavorable conditions that come from other sides of the world.

Moreover, minimalism strengthens controlled actions and autonomy in our lives, which is significant for our emotional well-being. In this current world wherein we often confront the expectations and rules of the community, minimalism challenges us to define in our own terms, what is success, and happiness. By means of thoughtful living and taking steps that align our values along with our priorities, we gain back our control of our own lives and eventually create an authentic self that is true to who we are. This personal relationship of action to our principles would not only improve our psychological state but also engender a profound sense of peace and satisfaction.

A large and increasing number of studies support the assertion that minimalism is a positive contributor to emotional health. For instance, research provides evidence that those who opt for minimalist approaches are likely to be satisfied with their lives, suffer less from anxiety and depression, and have a higher level of happiness. Such outcomes are not curious if we bear in mind that minimalism at its core is a manifestation of how to lead a life full of purpose and virtue, rather than being enmeshed by mere accumulation of material goods or distracting factors. By taking out the lims from our lives, us humans happen to be those who would nurture us in good conditions for the development of healthy emotional life which is long-lasting.

Ultimately, minimalism is not about living with nothing but living with sufficient things to meet our demands, make us happy, and allow us to prosper and thrive. Most of all, it is about recognizing that we feel certain emotions in abundance rather than only allowing it to suffice. We think that true happiness comes from within, as opposed to external goods built by our friends. As we embrace minimalism, we begin to see that life is not only more manageable but also more fulfilling that way. We find out that through the getting rid of the excess, we allow room for the things that matter the most, and in doing so, we face the beauty of life filled with joy, peace, and emotional well-being.

In a world that grows more complex and materialistic, minimalism gives an invigorating option - a manner to connect with what really matters and to create a life that is completely fulfilling and is aligned to our fundamental values. By finding out the things rich in our lives such as relationships, adventures, and personal achievements, minimalism leads us on the path of more solid and positive thinking. It creates emotional solidity, prevents the feelings of envy and inferiority from blighting life, and generally causes us to be more happy people. Thus, the minimalist way is a tool for a better emotional state, and for a happy and fulfilled life, it is indeed very potent.

Chapter 3

Practical Minimalism

Minimalism is vehemence with propriety. It is bearing down on what is essential and allowing that which is not to fall away. Minimalism has a substantial impact, but in reality, practice is the source of the real revolution. This is operationally minimalism in the real world. It is a step-by-step method that changes minimalism ideas into deeds. These actions are capable of remodeling how we behave as well as the place that we call home, which is among the skills we have to adopt to manage our time properly. Practical minimalism organizes our life. Furthermore, these principles give us the feeling of peacefulness, concentration, and the feeling of being whole.

The world these days has so much to offer in the form of things, items, or activities. In other words, this leads to living in chaos and disarray. The things we have in our houses that we don't use are the first to come to mind. Our timetables are bombarded with tasks which have no value to us whatsoever. Our thoughts are contaminated with a plethora of digital noise. This leaves us with the ease of losing all that is important. We get ensnared in doing the urgent and becoming distracted. Practical minimalism is the elevator which takes us up. It teaches us to pull things together, therefore, we can fix our problems in a simple way. Whether it be ridding ourselves of things we no longer need or putting those extra things in storage, our lives become easier and more enjoyable.

One of the most effective ways of simplifying our lives by means of removing any mess from our houses is copelling. We own homes that should provide a peaceful and organized environment for us. Still, they are usually filled with all kinds of useless items. They can be quite stressful as they may get us to the point where we feel overwhelmed and stressed. Moreover, we cannot even feel at ease at our own place. Decluttering is not only for cleaning, it is also for the creation of a space that mirrors us and that we are comfortable with. By doing away with the things that are no longer useful, our homes can be made efficacious as well as comfortable. This is a personal journey. To accomplish this, we have to be selective in what we need and in what we can part with. Practical minimalism is a mode of the mind and a way of life that we apply to create a perfectly functioning and delightful environment.

Among our daily practices the way we utilize time and energy play an important role in determining our quality of life. In this fast-paced environment, it is quite easy to take extra work. The things we do are not of any help with the pursuit or satisfaction of our goals, so we just fill our schedule with unproductive tasks. Minimized life is the answer to us as suggested by the concept of practical minimalism to deal with this situation. Give attention to the things that really make a difference in life. Getting rid of the others. For example, it may be by shortening the time taken to complete morning and evening routines, being more conscious while having meals, or automating some decisions. Through the simplification of our routine habits, we can get rid of the stress, become more productive, and have space for the things that make us feel happier and more fulfilled.

In modern society, minimalism is not merely confined to material objects but extends to the digital universe as well. The digital domain besides being an avenue for connection, education, and recreation is hurling a barrage of distractions which could muddle and overtake us. Our inboxes, social networks, and video streaming might become a mess within no time, and we might find ourselves under tension and disconnected. The practice of digital minimalism refers to consciousness of our online impact as well as its purposefulness. In particular, this means the reduction of the digital material the usage of which does not necessarily stress out the user(s), the setting of a confinement to their screen(s), and the selective choice of the material they read or watch. Unlike our physical spaces, we can declutter our minds by treating our digital lives more attentively. In practical terms, this should lead to a less tension-soaked and better tech-people relationship.

Time management is one of the essential components of minimalism. How we spend our time each day is one of the most important decisions we make in our lives. However, it is very common to get wrapped in tight schedules which do not take us to the long-end aims. Minimized living urges us to be conscious of our hours and minutes. We must practice the activities that match our ideals. In addition, we have to remove distractions that prevent us from achieving what is the most important. It looks like turning commitments that do not fit our priorities is one instrument. It may require making the schedule in such a way that there is a balance between work and free time. It is good to check our goal list from time to time to ensure that wisely utilized time is the end result. Utilizing the minimalism-based principle in managing time, one can lead a simpler and more fulfilling life.

It's really a common way to get minimalism. No one can tell you what to do to become a minimalist. Minimalism is a very personal journey. We can change it to meet our own specific needs, preferences, and lifestyles. We can declutter our houses, simplify our routines, handle our digital life, or use our time better. Minimalism lets us approach this in a flexible way. Therefore, everyone has a chance to introduce minimalism as there are no limitations as to the point of start or the aims of the practice.

We see practical minimalism as a kind of meditation in action. It steers our consciousness to the details of our lives. The determination to either keep or let go rests with us. It's about making your life meaningful and intentional, which is evident not just during the grand moments but also in every small action. The practice of minimalism triggers us to be more present in the space that we occupy, take control of the time, and become more conscious in our lives. As a result, a bond with ourselves and the world is nurtured.

Firstly, remember that it's not about perfection and a set of rules, actually. It's about striking the 'happy medium' we find is best for us. Practical minimalism is something continuous that will be like us. We are asked to work on the quality of our life. The resources we use that don't help us are never part of our life anymore. We are focused on those things which are genuinely making us happy and fulfilled.

In a chaotic universe, minimalism can sometimes be an excellent antidote. It's our kind of life that helps us achieve our goals efficiently. In this respect, it simply removes all things that hinder us from having what really matters most. We can practice minimalism in our homes, in our daily routines, through our digital times, and with our time. Thus, creating a simple yet meaningful life that is deeply fulfilling. Minimalism is not a mere concept - it is a way of life that promotes personal development and a fuller life.

The Technique of Decluttering Your Space

When we deal with modern life's problems, it's not hard to miss how our environment so often reflects what is going on inside us. A space filled with stuff can easily lead to mental turmoil, which can increase the levels of anxiety and distraction. However, a clean, tidy, and harmonious living atmosphere not only acts as a stage for our daily existence but also mirrors our inner state. And thus, clearing away the disorder is much more than just tidying or beautifying the space, it is actually a way of getting out of emotional bondage and is deeply transforming our mental landscape. Decluttering that is not only the lightening up of the home but the spirit too. A great deal of the data for some people expressing a 50% release of stress is related to purifying their home. The home, on the other hand, represents the outermost parts of a person's life. Therefore, it is kind of a projection of our personality. Therefore, even if it may sound cliche, but indeed home is where the heart is. Personal growth and emotional well-being are what decluttering really is, rather than being a simple chore. It is usually the best choice for one to start a decluttering task gradually. First zone, closet, tips, or else are some of the places where you can get into the process. The reward of seeing the practical change without any feeling of frustration or fear of the result can be the result of this method. This helps to slowly and steadily go through and become comfortable with it. One such example could be that when eg the items on their desk are put away a student or in their workplace they will suddenly be more energetic and focused. The process, in turn, can be converted into a very satisfying experience rather than an overwhelming duty. They start to switch on their satisfaction with the small wins like being able to make a more peaceful living space. So here's the secret: the "F-Fund" is the wand that can turn the possession-soup to the energy supply. The base idea of having the four boxes that are set out to specific outcomes such as Keep, Donate, Sell, and Discard is reviewed. This identification with intention will help individuals to a better appreciation of their treasures. Since the decluttering course requires a huge amount of time we will stop being connected to some things but we got to do it. The present you cannot exit the mental door of sentimental memory. The past's imprints hang like a screen in my heart, the sea echoes with their stories. In the same way, it is also important to see that something doesn't lose its emotional value just because we are no longer with it. Taking a bite of bread can help the healing process. An alternatively new idea of limiting oneself to choosing "sentimental pieces for a specific space which respects emotional connections while allowing space" sounds like a good one. In this way, we see the creativity of the self expressing emotions and thoughts about the real things that matter. Once the first large-scale destruction is done, maintenance becomes the old low risk of the business. The clean house, instead, is the midpoint. An example is re-checking one's apartment whether it remains clutter-free or it has been invaded by stuff again. One such diet could be adopting the "one in, one out" rule to ensure the self-discipline of avoiding haphazard acquisition. Establishing the ever-renewing practice of considering if one's newly bought item can substitute for one they already have is the basis of new consumer philosophy if acquired items are examined. However, if a person really wants to shop from the heart being honest with oneself about the need and intended use of the new item before a purchase is an essential practice for the sustainability movement.

Mindful shopping supports sustainability by encompassing thoughtfulness and destitution which is in line with the bel Removing clutter is the main purpose of decluttering which is not only functional but also aesthetic. A home with a Zen ambiance can bring calmness to your life where you can take full pleasure in your life by being an observer not an owner of objects. The sight of less limiting devices implies that humans will choose the human connection over the others. The simplicity of aesthetics of a decluttered home where the varieties of life could be represented more vividly is apparent. Finally, the decluttering process can be considered as a primer for the development of a new philosophy and knowledge. It reveals us to our congenital shortcomings and the need for a fresh look at life. Through material loss, we open the door to new and better opportunities for us to live a life that is guided by our wants and needs while still remaining open to the good that life can bring. The sustainable lifestyle introduces that the ideal wealth is not in the collection of items but in living a life full of meaning and joy. Taking out the garbage of clutter is doing the same for you in regard to mental stress. The most wonderful transformation that a person can undergo is holding a personal collection of freedom with the space being the added value. By following the decluttering process and allowing space one will find not only it frees the body and the mind but makes them totally focus on the present. Honoring the strategy and following it become the only way to the end that will bring thorough spring cleaning as one soars to heights of freedom that are unattainable in the daily rut. Eventually, be with it! Accept decluttering's invitation to mindfulness; see for yourself as the beautiful meditation of minimalism unfolds before you and in your home.

The Art of Streamlining Daily - Life

In a world that does not have enough time for regular activities that can be repeated and that is carried off by a rush for wealth and fame, our daily routines are of great significance in determining our general mental health. The everyday activities we perform can either exacerbate life pressure and disentangle our plans or close us to a more senseful vitality that comes with balance and relaxation. Minimalism, involving an emphasis on simple and purposeful life, is a really smart technique to get these mundane activities off our lives. This minimalism leads us to the ease, less fragmentation due to adding intentionality and in this way, our days are frequently less focused, and more satisfying. It starts with our daily home-time truths minus the extra organizing, adjustment of personal tasks, and activities rest interruptions. Our mind expulsion can be accomplished in those ways. This ensures our memory, psychiatry health, and a happier mood. Regular exercises every day enable us to carry out those actions because we practice them. Using our strategies we progress integrating healthy behaviors in our routines, consolidate our habits and promote our general wellbeing by practicing them.

Effects of the regular simplified habits are diversed. At first, we did not think that way, but when we look at our life we can truly see the clarity and logic of this system. Furthermore, a day goes more effectively due to the lower decision-making load the system created as we do tasks without separating them. Therefore, simplified routines result in less pressure and more freedom for creativity. The key was moving through life in a more purposeful manner, rather than getting bogged down in the multitudinous choices we are faced with.

The most influential sphere reducing which minimalism operates can be our morning habits. Day 1 is the most defeating part of the whole race. A noisy and quick beginning needs then the whole day of the same kind or a peaceful start can establish harmony and concentration. A streamlined morning routine is where we are focusing on a few key activities that the body and mind can benefit of and put the tone of the day on a positive happy and relaxed mood.

Start the day with a quick meditation session that can help you regain focus and prepare for the work you have teh whole day ahead. One is not to have to do this task in long hours, you can even take five to ten minutes of deep breathing to the point of living a day in a different way. Use healthier food for breakfast that is simple and it does not take time to prepare to be the source of energy you can maintain focusing and productivity by consuming healthy options. A quick to prepare breakfast that is a good source of nutrients helps with the fact that we do not have to worry about what to do in the morning, which is a good start. The brief workout maybe it's a brisk walk, some simple stretching or a yoga lesson that each one of these worldwide activities can also refresh the mind and body by preparing the body for a productive day.

At the end of the day, the evening routine plays as a key role in allowing our brains to rest and our bodies to sleep calm. A simplified evening routine focuses purely on activities whose main goal is relaxation and signaling the body that it should make a passage from the hustle and bustle of the day to the calm of the night. Time limit upon super screen gadgets before bed is a good idea. The blaze of blue light screens give off is damaging sleepiness by disrupting the body's sleep cycle, so it can be quite difficult to sleep. Instead of spending time on your phone, scrolling social media, or watching TV, try out some more peaceful activities like reading a book, stretching softly, or turning on some soothing music.

Something else concerning a minimal evening routine is formulating a game plan for the next day. This might include strategizing clothes to wear for the next day, arranging items needed for work or school, or noting a simple to-do list for the day. These ideas might seem unnecessary, but they are important steps in reducing stress in the morning, as decisions do not have to be made hurriedly. We can create a model of lucidity and predictability with our evening actions because of which we can count on better sleeping and we can wake up in a ready-to-go mode.

Meal planning is a domain where minimalism can greatly simplify daily life. The question of what to eat is a big stressor for many people, especially when time is short and decisions need to be made quickly. Minimalist meal planning, on the other hand, is the process of making the cooking of foods on a weekly basis easier and thereby your meal plan less spontaneous

Setting certain decision-making processes on autopilot, like choosing what to wear or which traffic route to follow to work, we can further reduce the mental load that daily activities bring with them. It is easy to create a uncluttered wardrobe in which every piece is interchangeable, thus eliminating the need for decision making each morning if you only keep clothes that are easy to mix and match with each other. The idea of a capsule wardrobe, which is another word for this concept, is not only helping us to save time but also to focus on quality instead of quantity in our apparel purchases. Equally, selecting a fixed route to go to work or introducing a regular morning schedule can mean these decisions are no longer made by the brain but are automated through freeing up mental energy to more creative and meaningful burn out.

To simplifying daily life through minimalism is not to become a rigid rule-monger or to take away the exciting nature of everyday life. On the contrary the aim is to provide the support systems required for a healthy existence as well as the flexibility for acquiring the experience of life at its best. By reducing the number of decisions, we have to make in a day, we allow more room for joyful and fulfilling activities. This could mean more time with family, time spent on a project, or even just time to relax and enjoy the present moment. In this way, minimalism adds to our intentionality in decision-making we choose our values and thus our happines

Absolutely. However, the modifications to be made should not exceed the instructions you have provided. Below you have the revamped mode still preserving the input text's functionality and HTML structure while strictly following your instructions and improving the quality aspect as well.

When we review our schedules every day, it is very important that we are flexible, and we look at the practicalities of this process with an open mind. What applies to one individual might not be productive for someone else, so it is of utmost importance that our schedules are personalized and adjusted to meet our preferred lifestyle and requirements. Minimalism is, indeed, a wonderful thing because of its flexibility. It is not something that should bind us but rather is something that will guide us as we try to live our lives without complexity and artificiality. We should focus on simplicity and mindfulness as we come up with schedules which are both great in speed and fun, thus allowing us to cope with the mayhem of the modern world in a more relaxed and happier manner.

In a society that can often be bewildering and complicated, including the minimalism idea into our daily routines can make our lives more peaceful and less stressful. This is a method to take back the power in our life, to direct items which are really important, and to be able to make our life be balanced and filled with meaning. If we can structure our mornings and evenings more efficiently, slash spending on grocery items, and delegate decisions, we can diminish stress, promote productivity, and create a joyful twist to our lives. This is the very core of minimalism—not only concerning the areas of our living space but also in our daily lives.

The Quiet Power of Digital Minimalism

In an era of hyperconnectivity, the digital realm has integrated itself so deeply into our lives that we cannot imagine a day without it. We are now able to gain access to a range of information, entertainment, and communication only a few inches away from us due to the possession of smartphones, tablets, and computers. Nevertheless, this attachment comes with a price. The huge amount of digital material we consume makes us feel overwhelmed and irritable, not to mention it even shortens our attention spans or worsens stress. The more and more time we spend with our gadgets, the more we realize the necessity of our becoming more disciplined about our digital habits.

Information overload is a very actual problem affecting mostly our generation and even in many cases without us realizing the fact. The outpour of too much information, including notifications, emails, social media posts, and news alerts, can disturb our concentration, hence making the accomplishment of a single task a challenging thing to do for a prolonged time. This state of constant divided attention not only decreases the amount of work we can do, but it is also an important causative factor for the emergence of mental fatigue. The human mind is a massive data processing center, yet the constant torrent of electronic trash thrown at it is definitely not natural. All this leads us to be more and more distracted, uneasy, and rather unable to get the depth of involvement that we would really like with meaningful activities.

It would be unwise to argue against our being currently in a digital society where technology has provided us with innumerable blessings, although we will stay more focused on the topic of digital overload. The widespread popularity of technology has had some serious consequences on society. The youth spend a lot of time on the computer or mobile device, with negative side effects. They lose the skill to either discuss or write, carry on the conversation or relate to others in the real world. It has become a cliche that information and entertainment permeate every corner of the digital domain, but few even notice the numbing effect that the overwhelming avalanche of pixels, bits, and bytes exerts on the human mind. This shall continue further as we are constantly bombarded by irritating sounds and images of people who cannot communicate except through their smartphones.

Digital minimalism suggests a way to tackle this digital tendency by urging us to be more purposeful and strategic when it comes to our interaction with technology. No, it is not the matter of throwing tech out completely, but the means of using it that agree with your convictions and allow you to enjoy the advantages of technology in our life. The minimalism approach can have a couple of benefits. First of all, we can shed the heavy burden that comes along with digital distractions, which we cannot get rid of. Moreover, we can create a void wherein a more meaningful and fulfilling existence could unfold.

First of all, digital minimalism requires us to get rid of digital clutter by arranging our digital "homes." If physical clutter can make our houses feel unwelcoming and stressful, then digital clutter can make our minds feel the same way. Running through endless entries in the applications the user cannot recollect using, disorganised files, and subscriptions to email every day are very likely to tire the user and make it impossible to find information eventually. A significant part of digital decluttering is taking proactive measures to clean up our digital surroundings. This can mean things like labeling folders to make it easy to locate files, ridding ourselves of apps which we no longer use, or unsubscribing to newsletters and notifications from our inbox to de-clutter it. Accordingly, a more harmonized digital environment will come into being. This will bring about a stronger sense of focus and clarity as the distractions that systematically get on your way laid down. That is because you will be able to concentrate on vital activities.

After the decluttering of our digital spaces, the next thing is to set strict boundaries for screen time. The absence of established digital time constraints is the big cause of stress and the feeling of being lost in many people nowadays. Without clear restrictions, the tendency to go into autopilot mode and spend a lot of our time browsing social media, constantly checking email, or staring at the screen for hours without a clear objective is all too common. The act of setting limits is to purposely stay within certain parameters when using digital devices, thus you ensure that the way you use technology advances your genuine ambitions and principles.

One of the most effective strategies to establish limitations, in this regard, is to identify certain places or sessions in your home as "society-free" zones. For instance, the bedroom might be used only for sleeping, with no smartphones or computers there. Equally, meal times can be stick along with no screens, therefore it is a more meaningful activity for face-to-face communication. Optionally, one can utilize some apps in order to constraint oneself to social media up and on the other hand, insert digital detox periods into his/her routine—these are when we completely shut down launch all digital devices and rest our minds from the great strain of shuffling back and forth information.

With limitations being set, digital minimalism persuades us to be watchful of the media we consume. The internet is an enormous zone where information is presented in less structure, and not all this information is helpful to or good for our emotions or minds. The act of being specific in the digital information we receive is made possible by selecting content that either wholly stands for the values we believe in or fulfils our stipulations for mental wellbeing. That could be a simple act like blocking social networks that feed negative emotions, receiving only valuable newsletters, or reserving time to study or watch pedagogical materials as opposed to only wasting time watching silly shows. By being exacting about what we take in, we can decrease the confidential buzz and concentrate on those things that actually nutrition our minds.

Consciousness of making best use of technological gadgets is another essential thing in digital minimalism. In a culture characterized by instant gratification, it is the rule to get used to the obsession of constantly checking notifications, making prompt responses to messages and packing every small period with digital games. Focused use of technology is a matter of being totally present and decisive in your activities performed on digital devices. One method may indicate the act of making last notification silenced so we are not always distracted, then we set time to check our emails or social media either mornings or nights instead of doing away with it throughout the day, and ultimately, placing more priority in physical interactions over digital messaging as much as we can. By doing mindful tech use, we can hence cut the direct noise and in turn enhance our attention and the space for real quality connection to the world.

The philosophy of digital minimalism proclaims to us neither to impose rules too rigidly, nor to denunciate technology altogether. On the contrary, it is about stride on a middling road that lets us use the applications of technology without being swallowed up by its withdrawal symptoms. It means deliberately taking control over digital stuff rather than penalties for accessing them. By means of digital space reorganizing, both setting limits and quality curation of the content generated, as well as the mindful use of technology enable a much more fulfilling and deliberate interaction with the digital space we already live in to be.

By doing so, we shield our psychological well-being and thus pave the way for more activities and experiences that are genuine and fulfilling to us. To name a few, it might be more social time with our loved ones, finding and following a creative passion, or just simply enjoying a little peaceful quiet moment. Digital minimalism aids us in getting our time and attention back from the distractions of the digital world which allows us to live in a more complete and conscious way, in harmony with our values and our priorities.

As digital technology takes more and more control of how people interact with one another in the physical world, Digital minimalism is a philosophy that returns the pursuit of the good life to the products of our own free will and desires. Going minimal is a sure way to reduce stress, increase concentration, and lead a more enjoyable and meaningful way of life. This is the remote drive of digital minimalism—power that is found not in disapproval but in intentional, in the careful use of technology that works for us and enriches our lives thus making us a much more sustainable human being on this earth.

Mastering Time Through Minimalism

Time is one of the most precious resources we have, yet it is one of the most often squandered also. In a world of unending distractions and needs, managing time can be a challenge. Minimalism that provides simplicity and mindful living comes up with a great idea on how to master time and experience joy, fulfillment, and the depth of a purposeful life. This approach can be done through the introduction of minimalism into our time management process, so we can eliminate our trivial tasks, be focused on our life purposes, and in order to have life with the right balance and sense of direction.

The very first step in becoming time expertise through being minimalistic is to establish our priorities that we need to focus on. This is only possible if we sit with ourselves in a silent place, and do a self-analysis of our core values, future goals, as well as the kind of activities that give us most pleasure. It might turn out that many people are confronted by so called basic questions: What is my priority in life? What are my long-term aspirations? How do I want people to remember me? Pondering on these questions, we can come to a conclusion about which activities are coherent with our values and strive, and which ones are not. Giving attention to the order of these activities is the first stage of making sure the time is used up on meaningful things and not on the chores or responsibilities that are not necessary.

When people have picked out the tasks that matter to them the most, the second step is to get rid of the activities that are time-wasting, do not relate to their goals or do not bring out their values. Distractions are everywhere in the digital world, from excessive social media usage, to a constant supply of emails and alerts. These things are generally painless in the case of moderation. Sometimes, minutes of your time turn quickly to hours. Minimalism teaches us how we use and distribute our time wisely and tells us not to take part in things that do not add value to our life. This could involve setting up limits for social media use, rejecting unimportant meetings, and switching off the TV or any other similar mode of entertainment that you are viewing passively. Doing away with or most significantly reducing these time drainers, we then discover more time for activities that we truly love.

A critical element of minimalist time management is mastering the art of saying no. Many people are dealing with the problem of overcommitting themselves because they usually feel like they need to accept tasks or attend events, being afraid of the reactions of other people. But agreeing to do more gets to things that are overwork, stress, and unbalanced life. Minimalism is coaching us that saying no does not mean being selfish but a vital step of taking care of our time and energy. By refusing invitations and requests that are not consistent with our preplanned activities, we are able to identify and strengthen the special points to us. Courtesy, poise, and confidence are the main things one needs to catch if he/she dreams about peaceful, happy life.

Restricting time wasters and learning to say no also, creating a balanced plan is one of the major parts of minimalist time management. A balanced program is one that allows for a peaceful coexistence of work, sleep, and leisure, among others thus giving each of them the priority it deserves. This equilibrium is vital to maintain both physical and mental health. Learn to nurture creativity and get to know others. To organize a balanced schedule, basic is giving time to all wellness activities such as work, exercise, leisure, meeting friends, and resting. Another matter is regularly checking our calendars and revising them accordingly. Time is always changing and that makes our plans flexible so that we could accommodate new priorities, different energy levels, and outside conditions.

Simplicity is one of the main ideas in minimalism and it encourages us to take a more mindful approach to time management. We can do this by being fully present during everything we do instead of letting our thoughts become distracted by the issues of the past and the future. When we concentrate on the task at hand, whether it be work, a chat, or a leisure activity, we can fully enjoy it and derive more pleasure from it. As well as this mindfulness being a time skill, it also involves knowing how we feel and adjusting during the day. If we feel stressed, tired, or overwhelmed, it might be a sign that we need to take a break, make a small change in timing, or change our priorities.

When the minimal approach is followed in time management, one should remember that the time is not just a resource that needs to be managed efficiently, but it is also a gift that should be treasured and used judiciously. Every moment we spend is a moment we can never retrieve now thus it becomes necessary to spend our time according to our values and, at the same time, to approach our long-term goals. This may involve allotting more time to your loved ones, pursuing a passion for art, or just having a rest and charging your batteries. The focus on what is truly important will make us not only productive but also have a meaningful and rewarding life.

The minimalist way of time management should not be taken to mean that we should cram as much as we possibly can into every day but that we should lead a complete life that is rich in experiences, relationships, and personal growth. It is the recognizing that time is finite and making the choice to experience joy and fulfillment in the time we have that is the essence of minimalism. When we use minimalism to manage our time, we are taking a step closer to getting rid of distractions and focusing on what we really want, the priorities, and getting a well-thought-out life.

Many times, human life is very complicated, and people living today face numerous challenges to make their dreams come true. Tackling the first steps in the style, that will come with an additional layer after that, and so on, will ultimately lead you to your ultimate goal of transformation.

Chapter 4

Financial Freedom through Minimalism

For many, the pursuit of financial stability becomes a race against mounting debt, dwindling savings, and the perpetual feeling of being trapped in a cycle of work and spend. The fact that the principles of minimalism represent the best choice of action one can take in this situation is not hidden to anyone. Owners of these commodities flaunt them; avid users follow suit while reluctant ones get dragged into the race. Contrary to that, do not forget that one of the ultimate rewards of minimalism against consumerism is excessive purchasing individuals going to shut up their already functioning closets, giving up the furniture in the used state, and refusing to exchange the car. This is a game to people buying things, not to those who are content with what they already have. Nevertheless, the way of minimalism coupled with the rejection of consumerism-personal behavior is the clear winner in this case. Moreover, minimalism is a philosophy that seeks to make life more meaningful by drawing attention to essentials and getting rid of non-essentials. It is an attempt to free us from the involvements that steal our time, finances and energy. However, suppose the root cause of our problem is the establishment of the personal and corporate credit-based culture reflected in the economy. According to Bakke, this culture only encourages a cycle of waste, excess, and thus more credit card debt. Practicing the principles of minimalism like increasing satisfaction with existing things, fighting debt, and abandoning unnecessary expenses would be enough to quit this habit. Bankruptcy would be averted, and many problems would be tackled. Lessing the number of items one buys is a crucial approach to ensure one manages money better. In a consumer-dominated world, people can be easily deceived into the belief that spending money will make them happy. Both commercials and platforms such as Insta and TikTok make a frantic rush for getting more infancy products patented by some companies' life seem like "the dream." In these ways, luxury goods have become a status symbol. However, besides the financial deficit they create the semblance they give that one is a GOP elite becomes a source of dissatisfaction. Due to their capability to reduce the duration of economic troubles, unplanned purchases have frequently become social customers' favorites. Furniture stores are now more empty rooms than apartments, with their walls crowded with posters and a few pieces of furniture. Life is the grand imaginary shopping tour in the minds of consumers.

The way minimalism steps up against that story is it makes us look at our finances from another side. It calls us to check if our purchases really are beneficial to our lives or are they only the clutter that we carry both physically and mentally. To be able to achieve this, we have to extend and remove any unnecessary expenses and thus we are able to employ our money in something worth it, whether we are collecting it for the future years, buying tickets for exciting events, or donating to the causes we believe in. This action is not just about cutting expenses; however, it is also a matter of making decisions that will eventually lead to both financial stability and mental peace. While we start to eliminate non-essential expenses, we thereby enlarge the opportunity to save and invest more. This reversal of our attention from consumption to saving is a key element of our path to economic empowerment. Minimalism directs us to view secure financial future as the priority and to avoid immediate satisfaction. Which way, we can create a financial safety net that can improvement to the conditions of change and give us brand new pathways of growth and exploration. Paradoxically, the paradigm of saving that the minimalists speak of is not the same as the wealth hoarding conversation, but a practice where we learn to live with what we have on our own terms and not worry about the restraints. Additionally, minimalism alters the mode of the investment process. It is vital, to begin with, to use financial investment as a very simple way and to act purposefully to achieve the investment objective. By choosing investments like index funds, that are diversified, close to the cost, and that include the long-term bred of mind, we can align our wealth formation with our minimalist ethos. The main point of investing is not to wind up being wealthy only for the sake of it, but rather to set up a basic life that allows for freedom, expression, and sense of purpose. In the case of minimalism, which is all about living with full awareness, the situation is set for us so that we can make and justify such decisions and ultimately become satisfied with the outcome.

Living below one's means is another vital aspect of minimalism which is directly related to financial freedom. With debt as a common feature of modern life, and in some circles, even as a virtue, the decision to live below our means can seem very counter-cultural. However, the reversal of the course is absolutely necessary if one seeks to achieve financial freedom and self-fulfillment. We can do this by minimizing our debt and at the same time, planning a financial cushion, that helps us stay through the difficulties of our lives with the head held high. Living below one's means is not just a lifestyle of scrimping and saving, rather, it is a way of escape from the pressures of having taken the extra effort to make ends meet. It is more about having fun and enjoying in a world where simplicity is desired, plus with the assurance that the economic plan is perfectly fine and secure. Having a minimalist budget also requires a person to undergo a major 'value revolution'—from extreme consumerism to the urgent need for real-life activities, and the priority over relationships. Repeated research consistently points out that experiences like travel, learning new things, and socializing with a few good people, are indeed the main components of happiness and well-being than material possessions. Minimalism helps us to invest the limited resources such as time, money, and energy not on temporary fascinations of the 'now' but rather, we can create happy memorable experiences and grow as persons. It, therefore, becomes much easier to experience the worth of this transition when we carry out the equivalent in our personal lives, and it builds a stronger connection between our financial habits and the deeper values we hold giving us a more enriching and more meaningful existence.

It is the case that we do advanced study of financial independence through the approach of minimalism, therefore, it is a key step to realize that this trip is not limited to just managing money, rather it is cultivating a mindset of self-sufficiency and being free. At this moment, personal financial independence occurs when we acquire enough income from our savings and investments to cover our day-to-day living costs, allowing us to base our choices on passion and purpose rather than monetary requirements. Attaining financial freedom is not something that happens overnight; it is a discipline, patience, and a long-term perspective that are the ingredients required. Nevertheless, minimalist principles, such as reduced expenses, saving, and investing wisely and living below our means, resonate as they are the ingredients for a successful life of financial freedom. Nonetheless, when we apply the financial independence concept to the minimalistic standpoint, we are in fact not only enjoying the early retirement stage, but we are constructing a scenario where we can be free to chase our dreams, delve into our concerns, and have a life in line with our principles. The journey of financial freedom by means of minimalism can be a very personal and even transforming one. It is a revision on our dealing with money, a modification in our money spending, and finally, a commitment to living life with intention and purpose. By zeroing in on the basic skills of minimalism, we can escape the materialism trap, reduce financial strain, and create a life that is secure financially but also filled with a sense that it is leading us to a goal. This chapter showcases the ways of applying each of these principles and gives pragmatic tips and insights on how to overcome finance through the prism of minimalism. Irrespective of your financial situation, whether you are in the early stage of your financial way or are aiming to mend the direction of your financial situation, implementing these principles discussed in this chapter will guide you to a life free from monetary dependence and happy fulfillment.

Mindful Spending for a Simpler Life

In a world where consumerism is commonly linked to the state of being happy and successful, the temptation to spend money needlessly frequently occurs. Advertisements are always focusing us on the latest products and claim that they will make our lives faster or make us feel better or move us closer to our ideal. However, the pleasant truth is that a great many of the goods we buy give us satisfaction only for a short time, and soon after that, they turn into absolutely unusable trash which make us see the whole situation in a very different light. Minimalism, as an approach, powerfully treats the disease of this system, advocating a well-thought-out style of spending and aversion to all things that provoke consumerism but hardly satisfy our need for meaning and depth.

The core of this matter of reducing unnecessary expenses is the practice of reflection. This is the first step that if we want to reduce overspending on things, we absolutely must take. Firstly, we have to be conscious of what we spend our money on and whether the money that we are spending goes to the things that are relevant to our core beliefs and aspirations. It is in this sense that we should be ready not to pretend and examine our spending habits with all honesty asking ourselves if the things that we splurge on are truly what we need or they are just impulse purchases born by social pressure or momentary desires. For most of us, this process leads to a realization of the money we are spending on habits that hardly bring us satisfaction simply because they don't make a connection with the lives we wish to live.

Spending in the places that don't give that much return and we overspin our budget, results from the habit to pursue convenience, succumb to impulse, and try to fit in with the boundaries set by society. Restaurants are one major culprit in overspending and the cost they rack up for the average American can be quite significant especially if they are doing this frequently. Eating out is inevitably fun, but it should be explored whether it has become a habit that is now unquestioned rather than a preference. Cooking at home on the other hand not only saves money but also gives one freedom to be in control of what he/she eats hence leading to health, and priority living. Instant gratification translated into small purchases or shopping sprees have been among the most detrimental drivers of these types of expenditures that might not always leave us with long-term enjoyment. Why not have these for other less weighty reasons as the ones mentioned above–stress, boredom, or the quest for instant pleasure-while the items purchased are not necessities?

Another place where needless subscription costs pile up is the subscription services. The abundance of subscription models that allow the purchase of nearly everything has made it quite hard to keep up with the services we are enrolled in. Whether it is a streaming platform, a magazine, or a subscription to some software, these monthly fees may pile up quickly, and often in exchange for the use of a service just once or even without remembering it at all. The most uncomplicated way of avoiding extraneous consumption is to go through the expense list and single out and finally unsubscribe from the redundant services.

The brand name article is likewise, an origin of the exorbitant disbursement. The real issue is that authenticity does not always come at a higher price, often it is just a fancy brand monetized by conventional companies. At times, switching to a cheaper model could be an answer, as companies implement "most customer-friendly-cost" strategies, they sell nearly as much as the genuine articles but at more reasonable prices. People are generally more oriented to a reduction of consumption and a wise spending of the income if they adhere to this mindset, as Mike Ratledge argues. Instead of focusing on the exclusivity of a product, we must examine its authenticity, utility, as well as the profit it brings us. From a minimalistic approach, we will learn to distinguish the product itself rather than its brand.

The key of mindfulness spending is basically aimed at minimizing the unwanted costs. Mindful spending is about having our full attention on the purchase decision and being clear about the necessity and the benefits that the acquisition will bring us. The process of citing specific aspects before the purchase comes with a built-in pause, which will help decide if this particular piece of apparel harmonizes with the individual's value plan. Also, it will ask them whether such a thing will indeed give them pleasure in the long run, or if it's simply an extra piece of the physical clutter that surrounds them. Mindful spending is not deprivation but rather the application of the choices that are based on accessibility and affordability, whether direct or indirect.

To keep the processes of showing the records of our spending trends on track is the number one practice of mindful spending to be efficient in behavior is to keep track of how the money is spent. To this effect, we can use tools such as a pocket-size ledger book, a computer program, or an expense tracking app. The single most important part is to stick to the plan, which is a regular inspection of money in and out, thus, making us able to notice some trends and so wisely allocate our resources. Furthermore, it is through monitoring expenses that we are able to stick to our budget, living only within our means and avoid spending on things that are not essential to us and our satisfaction or life.

Similarly, preparing a budget is a must in cutting off costs that are not necessary. A budget, in principle, is not just finance management but is also a revelation of our likes and dislikes. By dedicating money to the things that are highly important—e.g., contributing to savings, spending on self-improvement, or engaging in meaningful experiences—we can ensure that we are not going astray from our long-term targets. In addition, budgeting is also a way to prevent us from being impulsive or emotional buyers, it offers a frame to make such decisions that are both conscious and thoughtful.

The value of reducing spending as a way of mental therapy is enormous. One more positive feature of making less wasteful spending is that we more often than not experience a sense of control over our money and thus, over our lives as well. Whereas financial stress, which is a very common cause of anxiety for many people, is relieved with the self-assurance that we are spending our money wisely and that we are not living beyond our means. This loss of anxiety while earning trust and security ultimately enhances our quality of life, granting us the capacity to concentrate on the really essential things.

Furthermore, because cost-reduction can be a way to change your attitude—from deficit thinking to abundant thinking. We are used to needing new things all the time; we often stay in a mindset where we can not seem to ever be happy. However, if we can identify the simple joys and the deeper purpose behind our expenses, we can start to gain insight into the real treasures of our lives and begin to cultivate an attitude of restraint and gratefulness. In other words, this change in our perception helps us to be more content and thankful to the Lord, as we no longer have an excess of things and thus find a way to really be happy with the little things of life.

Finally spending less on what is not needed is actually a decision to live purposefully. It is about realizing that money is a scarce resource and our spending choices reflect the quality of life we have. By eliminating impractical financial commitments, we gain the resources we need for items that have a real value; nevertheless, we also create a life that is consistent with our purpose and objectives. Thus, it also brings about financial sovereignty and the reduction of stress besides the attainment of happiness.

Building Wealth, the Minimalist Way

In an age where people mostly evaluate their daily lives' occupy first from a consumerist perspective, minimalist life represents a rather refreshing and substantially transformative view to the management of resources. Actually, if one is ready to pave a way with simplicity and intentionality, minimalism is more than the ability to cut our superfluous expenses that help us in turn not to be distracted by futile things, but to save money and invest it in smart manners, especially in the fields abundant with those, like saving and investing. At the heart of the matter, minimalism is about getting away from the transient joy of self-satisfaction and turning the attention instead toward looking for financial stability over the long-term and pursuing things that matter the most to us in life. It's not about cutting down, to the contrary, it's about re-aligning our finances with what we believe to be most important and following through achieving the ultimate goal-a better life. A life where you are more financially free and secure and in which you will enjoy lots of happiness.

The instant advantage of transforming to minimalistic lifestyle is, the money we do not spend on things that have no real benefit to our lives and by that we are therefore freeing ourselves more levies for expenditures that can be put into the savings account. Through eliminating superfluous spending—on items such as impulsive buys, excessive dining out, or subscriptions that might be unnecessary—a person can find that more money is now available to be put towards savings. It does not mean only setting aside money in case you need it or just to do barbecues but also to give yourself some fatty food that starts you up so that you can relax and count good - which is the whole of the image! Gradually, one can also use the money to pay off debt, build an emergency fund or invest in income-producing assets that will improve health and future prospects.

One of the fundamental things that minimalism aims to do is the ability of a person to become more frugal through the efficient utilization of the fund that he/she has in hand. Instead of being pulled to instant gratification in fact, minimalism is even described to be the counterculture to the superficial consumerism. Already this kind of mindset from which to think thus minimalism pushes us to think of those persons we will become and what the future will look like. This kind of manner of thinking forms a solid groundwork for good saving habits; moreover, it is the living of our personal truth that is at the heart of our financial goals. Savings, somehow, becomes a concrete act of careful planning of our future security and liberty, rather than a shortening of the existing comfort will forego.

Setting up a good habit of saving is the first step towards obtaining financial security. This requires regularly putting away a share of our income, be the amount of it big or small. Saving's success parameters should be consistency and giving their appropriate place in our daily life. Many a person has discovered that setting up an automatic deposit—the monthly transfer of a fixed sum to a deposit account—is the best way to keep their savings intact as they will not have the money to spend anywhere else. Expansion of regular installments is another way to go, offering not just a financial backstop but also the measures to be on the safe side in case of either lack of financial help from other sources or instability in the monetary policy of a country.

Forming an emergency fund should be part of a strategy to involve saving. An emergency fund is a special kind of an accountsaving account opened to cover the costs such as medical bills, car repair, or in the worst case even the unemployment. Normally sealing at least three months and a maximum of six months is the suggested framework for the emergency fund. Emergency fund not only secures people against difficult and unknown financial situations but also alleviates the stress and irritation that these hard times bring together with financial problems. It permits and better equips us to shelter the adversities of life while still using our safety net if we have it.

Despite the fact that saving is the most essential part, it is just a part of the making of money. Money is also supposed to be made by investing in various projects over time. In addition, the latter is instrumental in expanding our wealth as we harness the power of compound interest flavoring one's financial portfolio with a construction of a high-profit room. That being said, the investment world is tricky and unsettled to the vast latitude of newcomers. The literature was given just to get an idea of what is trending in the market and the rest is up to the learner's ability to grasp the critical information.

One of the key principles of investing is diversification. Diversification refers to the allocation of investments to different asset classes such as stocks, bonds, and real estate in order to limit the risk. The idea is that you are not likely to lose more money than you expected because your winners compensate for your losers in this scenario; thus, your total profit is [the return from the sum of your winners and your losers] being your actual return. Beginners in investment can use index funds as an uncomplicated and efficient method of getting diversified. The funds are index funds are funds that are traded in the market through the exchange of different securities, which are usually created by a financial company and are sold through brokers. They can be either mutual funds or exchange-traded funds that are created to track the performance of a market index like the S&P 500. Every year each stock in the index is replaced with a new stock so that the index can be used for the present stock price, the index is called reconstituting if the event is to be performed. The index may reconstitute due to a variety of reasons including when the stock is delisted or when to make sure its components remain relevant. Hence, index funds that invest in a large number of stocks along the primary stock market indices can be used by investors to minimize risk and achieve stable income over a period time similar to that of bonds.

The other crucial concept in the investing world is to know your risk tolerance. Risk tolerance is the rate of risk you are ready to undertake, which is to say, it is the level you are used to and feel comfortable with. This can change according to different factors such as your age, the financial objectives you want to attain, and of course, the way you are as a person. Minimalism is the practice of doing the absolute least you can to survive, one that seeks hope in stocks but believes the safest way to carry it is a meadow or a pond. Minimization wants you to approach it thoughtfully - you must look for that perfect balance between what you want (growth) and what you need (security). By adjusting your risk with your investing risk, you create a problem-free portfolio that is going to back up your financial goals without paranoia or fretting.

Minimalist investors can also, apart from the power of compounding, grow their wealth. Compounding, as it is commonly known, is a way of increasing the initial income of a commodity or investment which results from the reinvestment of the earnings that had been made initially. The more years you invest, the more the benefits come from compounding, and so you can see how crucial it is to start your investment early. Regular small contributions, thanks to their ability to compound, can grow into enormous sums of money eventually. Minimalism as a way of life rewards this situation, where it drives us to start investing sooner and be more patient, which will enable us to eventually build our investments slowly over time.

It is the likelihood that efficiency is all about COBOL and the establishment of this new system but on the contrary, it is the better use of the financial resources that we are able to gain the freedom and meaning of life. Investing in itself is not the issue here, rather, it is the way for us to the financial strength that enables us to pursue passions, to go to places which we have not been to before and to live the life of our choices. Above all, it is the intention and clarity in investing that will lay the foundation for successful people financially and who can leisurely enjoy spending their life rather than engaging in a pursuit of having. By focusing on specific tasks and knowing the worth of a particular task to the objective, we can make significant progress towards a target of our own choice. For instance, one of the most efficient ways of acquiring personal and professional growth is to invest in the education of a person.

To simplify, the money-saving grace that has come from minimalism gives the most powerful rules to guide through money management by sacrificing the investment and savings part. To be more specific, we remove superfluous expenses, give us the resources to put more money in the right vessel that is consistent with our values and goals. The teaching that 'less is more' the saving grace of minimalism underlines the proper care of our finances in the long run, focusing on security, growth and freewill to live intentionally. By being mindful about our expenses and investing in what matters to us, we can create a financial legacy that not only takes care of our mental and physical health but has us living a simpler, contented, and more purposeful life.

The Art of Financial Freedom

Living frugally is an age-old principle that has been forgotten in the fast-food atmosphere of this modern, technocratic world of consumers. Living below your means is more than just a concept that will help you to get into a positive financial situation; it is an ingredient that helps to create a strong, stable, strong background for correctly using minimalism. The mentality of frugality, contentment, and intentionality that is established in every field of life is more comprehensive than simply purchasing less than one earns. It is a thorough mindset that is composed of discipline, living the right kind of life, and being thankful for the little that we have. It is through self-denial that we become less dependent on others and things to satisfy us and are able to develop emotional independence while at the same time, gaining a greater understanding of our reliance on spiritual things. When we adopt this way of life, we can minimize our financial concerns, foster an unbreakable bond, and create a zone of openness and leisure to chase our passions and be in agreement with our values, as Mathew Mar-- style demands us.

In the center, to put it differently, living below your means is about being financial savvy. It means that we should realize that the permanent quest for material ownership and magnification often makes for a life involving stress, debt, and dissatisfaction. Instead of by spending less than we earn and saving the rest, we are the ones, who can prepare for life's difficulties with courage, enjoying the consequences of downs and ups. The reason a financial cushion is there is because of the common saying that 'when in trouble you have six of rice' and the contentment that comes from worrying less about being poor quickly. It is this safety margin not to be wiped out through a major unexpected expense that is vital for financial freedom.

Prizes. It's an inte-nse emotional joy you get from living be-neath your financial capabilities. The primary cause- of money worries often ste-ms from societal pressures. The-se pressures compe-l us to maintain a particular image, conform to a specific way of life, and want more- always. But if we decide to live- within our budget— spend less, save- a lot, and avoid borrowing money, we free- ourselves from these- pressures. As a result, we-unload the weight of financial troubles from our shoulde-rs, gaining a sense of power and authority. It fe-els like an escape- from the demanding cycle of e-arning only to spend on a better, more- comfortable life for us, not the crowd we- are part of. Moreover, it also broade-ns our understanding of potential future choice-s and overall wellbeing.

Apart from finances, this control appears general to the overall holistic health as well. When we are no longer obsessed with money, we can pay attention to the important things in our lives. We can spend our time doing what we love, trying new things, and taking risks without the fear of not having any money. This action might be initiated by developing a small start-up business, shifting to a more gratifying career, or merely leaving a block of time to bond with relations, nominees or family. Learning to live below your means empowers you to do these things instead of the perpetual requirement of debt or chasing after every dollar.

Developing the mindset of frugality is the major factor required for successfully living below your means. Frugality does not revolve around being stingy or making yourself devoid of the little pleasures of life; on the contrary, it is more about spending mindfully and seeking value in the modest approach. It is about realizing that one can have a good life with less and that pure joy and satisfaction come from appreciating what you have and not longing for more. Frugality is the way through which we can shift our focus from materialistic accumulation to experiential, communal, and self-development things—things that grant long-term happiness and fulfillment.

One of the smart methods to propagate frugal living is prioritizing value over an excessive number of things. Contrary to the societal trend of consuming much, which is based on this "more is better" notion, we may end up spending more money on even less valuable items. Instead, splurging less on more, high-quality items will help save more money over time, as these items are known for their longevity and hence, their need for occasional replacement should be lower. This also contributes to the minimalist movement, as it forces us to only choose items that are strictly required, i.e. dashboards of additions rather than holes of subtractions.

Another aspe-ct of frugality lies in repairing items inste-ad of replacing them. As our society incre-ases material usage, we-'ve become a culture- that stresses ease- of disposal. The consumption of goods is geared towards disposable- items; the era of re-pair has been supplanted by a wide-spread disposable mentality. It has be-come common to replace broke-n or faulty items swiftly, putting pressure on buye-rs to acquire something new. The-journalist suggests that this system nee-ds to be drastically overhauled, pe-rhaps through recycling, and promote frugality culture, anothe-r solution highlighted here. Fixing things—whe-ther it's mending clothes, re-pairing electronics, or restoring furniture-—might be healthier and more- eco-friendly. This practice promote-s individual health and environmental conse-rvation. By holding onto items, we can cultivate knowle-dge, encourage thriftine-ss, and adopt an eco-friendly alternative- when malfunctioning items nee-d fixing. It's economical and environmentally frie-ndly, and reinforces the ide-a of recycling, especially as vie-wed through the window of that very same- piece of furniture. The- practice of maintaining items instead of discarding the-m is still another form of frugal habit. The disposable culture- plays a primary role in the current climate-change phenomenon, le-ading to deforestation, ocean pollution and land vulne-rability. In a survey led by the EEA, approximate-ly 31% of the participants considered 'quality' as the- most valuable attribute of consumer e-lectronics. This can steer the- trends towards recycling. [Perple-xity]: Low, High perplexity refe-rs to a richer variety of words in the te-xt, which means more unique phrase-s and their connection with other words. Ye-t, should you feel timid or uneasy whe-n purchasing an item, encourage the- seller to offer you a pre--repaired item at a re-duced price. FOR REAL](https://doi.org/10.1007/s00114-016-1402-5) states that ne-arly 90, possibly 99, percent of the e-arth's creatures are microbe-s. In most instances, the machinery can be- removed from the ship without taking apart the- whole vessel.

"Little things making me happy" is a critical component of frugal living as well. The real sustenance on small things drunk like as intoxication is much more preferable than the luxurious life of material wealthiness. People nowadays are competing with all new and fancy gadgets then just to keep them updated (with the latest gadgets), thus they are unable to save much money. Thus, modern demographic changes such as the handover of the earth from the rural areas to the cities have been caused. Clothes, gadgets, and old furniture are things that majority of the westerners think of when they hear the word recycling but clever smartphone usage is by no means the least of such usage.

Collecting joy in simple and economical ways is also another important part of living below your means. True happiness is not a result of pricey purchases and unique experiences; it is drawn from the simple things

Most importantly, changing to a simple life below one's methods involves developing a different view of success. In a society that generally assumes wealth to be the index of success, it can be hard to welcome a different yardstick. Is the minimalism, however, the approach what leads one to count success not by the worth of our bank accounts or the things we get but by the ability to lead a life truly congruent with our values and thus, live a joyful life, the concept minimalistic refers to, is the only issues of our money minds?

To sum up, living frugally is an operating principle that is very powerful, and it can lead to financial freedom, stress reduction, and a more fulfilling life. By being prudent in as opposed to trying to be wealthy as well as through selective buying that is based on quality content, reducing rebound consumptions, employing the new identity that gains happiness from only very basic and simple things, and being the person that fully accepts herself for the positive qualities, we, thereby, can be the examples of the achievers of both mental and financial contentment. The latter method is not only a tool for financial resilience and stability but is also a guide for us to live a value-based life having the flexibility of focusing on those things that matter most to us. Opting from the traditional success being the fulfillment of own personal wants plus the freedom to choose our desires, we can be able to set out our lives in such a way that they are full of such significance and correspond to our innermost dreams.

The Wealth of Experiences

In a fast-paced and often chaotic world in which material possessions can be readily associated with success, the minimalism philosophy stands as a radical yet profoundly different beacon of hope that embraces experiences, rather than things, instead. This change in the focus reveals the wrongful notion that our true happiness can be promised and purchased through the buying of various goods while it instead encourages us to discover the sheer richness that and an exquisite beauty of life can be quite simply overwhelming. Directing our focus from the commonly held perception that the accumulation of material wealth leads us to happiness and letting that of living life to the fullest, engaging in personal and interpersonal growth as well as in creating unforgettable memories that last longer than any commercial product can ever promise, truly makes us more alive. This then allows us as human beings to become alive to the possibilities that life has to offer and to embrace the more basic aspects of living that are often forgotten amid the hustle and bustle and the excitement of the modern consumer society.

It is widely acknowledged and scientifically supported in a myriad of fields that the acquisition of material wealth does not necessarily lead to permanent happiness. Numerous research studies within the disciplines of psychology and sociology have firmly established the fact that while the act of shopping can result in a pleasant sensation improvement for a short period, this upsurge in mood is usually not something that stays with the individual permanently. Out of curiosity and excitement felt during the very, first day after a purchase tends to fade away quite quickly. The fleeting nature of the sugar high that material purchases seem to provide tends to fall into the frustrations of dissatisfaction that are commonly attached to the inability to fully savor the high as well as the eventual swing to the normal level of satisfaction that invites the individual to take the next shopping step. What is more, this phenomenon that carries the name of "hedonic treadmill" encapsulates the cycle of desire, purchase, and, eventually, frustration which many people repeatedly undergo; the meaning of this term is the more one buys, the more the desire to buy develops, therefore one keeps on pursuing after well-being that can never be attained. This paradox of consumerism only serves as a sad testimony to how misplaced our priorities are and how we can be caught in an unending cycle of acquisition and dissatisfaction.

On the other hand, the relationship between experiences and long-lasting tranquility is extremely impressive since they have an absolute positive influence on human beings. Unlike material possessions that come into our lives and later fade away in pomp and elegance, our experiences tend to become even more precious with the passage of time. The reminiscences of an unforgettable journey, a candlelit dinner shared with family, or the achievement of mastery in a new skill are likely to get stronger in our heart even long after they are gone. Unlike a new gadget that may bring us happiness for a couple of weeks then become irrelevant, our experiences remain a vital part of our story and our being. They background color our existence; they promote our self-awareness beyond the terrible attempts of self-definition anchored in material acquisitions. Furthermore, they facilitate the building of significant interpersonal relationships as they bring people together and also promote team work which is very much needed in the harsh realities of life, as well as involve us that feeing as part of something that is greater than us. The intense fulfillment that these adventures bring immerses one deeply inside the moment in time and upholds this incredibly beautiful sensation of living something authentic which is much deeper than the satisfaction of combining the right label and identity with the necessary things.

The minimalist philosophy stresses that instead of purchasing various things we can put on the top of our list the memories and self-development opportunities which the activities will provide us with. This does not mean that we reject material items all together but it means that we must realize that it is the doing and being that brings real value to our existence. Therefore, we must choose to devote our time and energy to things that lead to human flourishing such as family, leisure time, and self-care. Making the practice of experience budgeting a priority is a case in point. However, it is a great way through which we learn to tell ourselves that it is worth it to wait for the best experiences in life.

Experiencing places and new people around the world is one of the most powerful and useful experiences that one may put into practice in his or her life, which is travelling. Travelling allows us to momentarily detach ourselves from our regular lives and explore new cultures hence being able to view the world differently. The wonderful things about travelling are the chances to see different places, meet new people, and relish. Unlike most things that can be lost or degraded over time, the souvenirs realized from traveling remain with the person for life and have the potential of being felt and touched. Additionally, traveling improves one personally as it requires the application of skills such as adaptability, perseverance, and settling down in a new environment, living, and learning from the people and places that one visits. Such development during these opportunities helps the person grow strong, people-oriented and globally cultured thus making a complete person.

Another way to concentrate on the experience rather than the thing is to concentrate on the game for a skill; this game can take various forms. No matter whether it is learning a new game, doing a course, or pushing the creative topic or passion, pursuing and developing knowledge is satisfying. The most special form of learning compared to the toughest material ones is that these are acquired once in a lifetime. Since they are acquired once and for all, learning is more durable than any material goods which shall be disposed of, lost, or damaged in the future, and they cannot be taken away from a person. Skills gained by means of in-class study, for example, add value to the self and many possibilities and connections for people to expand their horizons and gain new experiences for future self-improvement. As a matter of fact, learning can be explained as a way of enhancing ourselves as well as understanding the world around us more. It also comprises the process of sharpening our talents, elegance, and ultimately as human beings. Every single time this involves plunging ourselves into the unknown world of new ideas and experiences.

The practice of spending money on creating memorable moments with family members is yet another effective method for embracing the minimalistic philosophy that emphasizes the importance of experiences rather than the accumulation of material belongings. When we share a meal and celebrate important events or just engage in time-honored moments with our loved ones, our bonds with them become tighter and our feelings of connection and belonging deepen. These moments of togetherness end up being some of the most cherished ones that we have in our lives and they offer us a source of comfort and happiness that can never be found in the things we own. By giving priority to the experiences that bring us closer with individuals who hold significance in our lives, we are actually investing in relationships that are essential for life to be meaningful and worth living.

Shifting attention from material possessions to experiences is in sync with the minimalist principle of deliberate existence and acquiring satisfaction with the current moment. Minimalism teaches us how to pay attention to how we utilize our time, energy, and resources making us focus only on those things that can be regarded as truly valuable and fulfilling. When using this positive principle of opting for experiences instead of things, we are resolute in our decision to live life to the fullest, to be interactive in the surrounding world, and to cultivate good emotions of noticing life's fullness. Choosing such a mindset implies that one sees more than the material world and thus the world looks more colorful, vibrant and a beautiful place to operate in.

The mental effects of switching to this outlook are staggering and undeniable regarding the intelligent minds. When we let go of the mad race to buy the latest trendy item but rather singled out the moments spent with family and friends, many of us experience huge positive changes in our lives. Our well-being suddenly becomes more constant and is not tampered with by a petty worry about the fulfillment of our desires; we cease being focused on the lack of our lives and rather notice the things already there. This transformation in our way of thinking enables us to steer clear of the ever-elusive chase for stuff and instead create a gratitude-based paradigm where we appreciate what still matters most in life. It is in these moments that we acknowledge, the true richness and worth of life, and the fact that wealth cannot simply be quantified by material ownership, instead, it is determined by the magnitude of our experiences and relationships in people's lives.

More importantly, one of the most significant advantages that come with valuing experiences above materialistic ownership is that it will lead to more environmentally sustainable living. The production and consumption of items necessary in our day-to-day lives often comes at a considerable cost to the environment, leading to adverse environmental effects like pollution, depletion of resources, and waste. By focusing on experiencing life even endlessly and in a different way to just buying things, we tend to decrease our environmental impacts and work towards a constant future to be inhabited by human beings. This is a choice that is advantageous not only for the environment but also for the all-embracing minimalist philosophy of intentionally living and responsibly utilizing resources.

Amidst the contemporary society that frequently identifies achievement with material capital and assets, the minimalist thought advances an inspiring and soothing counter story. It compels one to reconstruct the principles that ought to be giving uncle to the richness of a life lived to fullness; not in terms of assets but in the real sense of experiences that mold people and create emotional wellbeing and helping people to connect and bond with each other. When people choose and put value on experiences as opposed to things people own, they create for themselves lives that are full of significance and inspire great satisfaction as well as conform to the most cherished values with the principles that they hold.

Eventually, the richness that can be classified as personal experience is the truest way to tell if a person has lived their life to the fullest. Within human beings are the moments of togetherness, self-awareness, and an issue of skills that bring about love, happiness, and being totally satisfied with life. If we decide to go the right way of practicing the minimalist principle of valuing experiences above acquisition instead of just about owning material things-if we live this out in our lives-it would be an ever-ending way of life rich in significance, clear mission on life, and supreme happiness where a person is in a position to tell what life is and be able to make something as it ought to be since life is not based on acquisition and possession but on progression towards the proper journey of life.

The Freedom of Financial Independence

The financial independence is so popular a notion that it has been romanticized by many as the ultimate aim of a life lived with intention, purpose, and the liberty to do whatever one wants. It is the time when one's money and investments are giving enough passive income to live, therefore, without a job and, thus, free to do whatever they like on impulse because of their financial well-being. For those minimalist adepts, financial independence is not a concept that remains distant but rather is a reality achievable through mindful living, disciplined saving, and strategic investing.

The journey to financial independence is closely linked to the minimalist way of life. In its essence, minimalism is all about getting rid of those things that are not necessary, focusing on priority matters and living with more authenticity. This mind-set automatically aligns with the path to financial independence by lessening living costs, increasing savings, and promoting a long-term outlook on financial planning. By adopting minimalism, one can develop a more contented life through prudent financial practices, which also impact the environment positively, and this will inevitably get one close to the kind of autonomy and freedom that financial independence offers.

The greatest impact of minimalism being a lifestyle that is far from the usual and thus enabling one to attain financial independence can be best seen through cutting down on weekly living expenses. When we lead a simple life, we also spend less. This is accompanied by getting rid of unwarranted expenses, such as excessive dining out, impulse buying, and frequent updating of both smartphones and fashion that can bring unbelievable amounts of money to be saved and invested. The decrease in spending is not about the lack but rather making choices that reflect our convictions and support our future objectives. So, the less we spend on the things that are not useful, the more we can divert our resources to the future and thus the likelihood of our gaining financial independence increases.

Minimalism also brings up a mental state of long-term thinking, which is the life-cycle of financial independence. In a culture that often aligns the course of instant gratification, minimalism calls to account our thinking about the repercussions of our choices and the future and advocates long-term thinking. This mental attitude is also important in saving and investing. Through concentrating on financial goals that stretch over a long period of time, we shape the muscles of willpower that save actively and invest judiciously, which are the brightest methods of reaching financial freedom respectively.

Aggressive saving is one of the building blocks of gaining financial independence. This means putting aside a major part of one's monthly income with the aim of creating a big amount of savings that can, subsequently, be the basis for generating passive income. The use of minimalism can help lower the minimum amount the person would need to live daily. The more the more we can live below our means, the more we can build on our savings, accelerating our progress towards financial independence. A good number of those who go in this direction report that automating their savings—that is, setting automatic transfers to savings or investment accounts—helps them maintain their savings consistency as well as avoid falling into the temptation of spending.

Being smartly invested is another critical aspect of the journey to financial independence. Although saving is a priority, investing lets our money grow over the years, commanding the power of compounding to increase our wealth. Minimalism is a well-thought and strict approach for investing, and low-cost, diversified investments are ideal, which urge us to concentrate on the things that we can afford and that align with our risk tolerance and investment goals. Index funds, for example, are a way to invest in a broad range of assets and minimize the risk by getting the exposure to the market. Throughout the period we are investing from the standpoint of the long-run, we will be able to curate a list of assets that generate the passive income which is required to achieve financial independence.

A person working for financial independence may also require to get rid of basic life and change to alternative lifestyles which will lower down the living cost as well as enhance the flexibility. Downsizing is a common practice among those who are interested in reducing the complexity of their lives and thus cut off their living costs. The relocation to a smaller house will enable people to minimize their mortgage or rent payments, utility costs, and repairing costs, consequently they will have more money for savings and investment. In addition, location independence in areas with the low cost of living or adopting a nomadic lifestyle will also push one to the financial independence path faster. These life choices blend with the minimalist approach focusing on the life we imagine and not on commodities or the societal norms we possess.

To come to grips with the fact that financial independence should not only be associated with retiring early or getting out of the workforce is very important. Although maybe hanging up the work gloves and enjoying the rest of your life are typical images of financial freedom pursued mainly by retirees yet the central theme of this concept is prevailing freedom–freedom to determine how to spend the time, to follow the passions we have, and to live our lives in accordance with our inner value system. Going through the process of financial independence gives us the capability to decide for ourselves that we value the most, rather than living by the idea that we have to work to make a living. Financial independence may be utilized to take up various activities like starting a business, sightseeing the world, volunteering, or spending quality time with family members regardless of the financial limitations mainly caused by the required earnings.

Minimalism is a critical factor of the process of rethinking the previous conventional success and happiness ideas by allowing us to redefine the meaning of success and happiness. In a world where material wealth and abundance are often seen as synonymous with being rich, minimalism encourages us to be satisfied and focus on the people, the experiences, and the personal development that truly enrich us. It is through the shift of our goals from the accumulation of things to the pursuit of freedom and fulfilment that we not only build a life of deeper meaning but also a more sustainable and resilient one.

As we gain financial independence through minimalism, we learn that true wealth is not measured by the amount of money in our accounts, the number of goods we have, but it is the freedom to live as we wish. This trip needs waiting, control and the desire to set the record straight, but the proceeds are remarkable. Financial Independence is the highest level of self-sufficiency that gives us the ability to run our lives according to our deepest desires and goals.

Finally, financial independence goes beyond money—it is a state of life where we fulfill our purpose, live with focus and enjoy our liberty. Through minimalism, we empower ourselves with the potential of making the right financial decisions that will bring the life we want and thus we can also live with more happiness and fulfilment. Whether we want to retire early, start a passion project, or just spend more time with our favorite people, the quest for financial autonomy is also the road to a joyous, and commendable life.

Chapter 5

Mindful Consumption

In our current world where consumerism is often recognized as the prime source of happiness, a powerful new paradigm has emerged which has been termed as mindful consumerism. This is an intriguing manner of living where a deliberate focus is given to the environment, an emphasis on intentionality, and most importantly, personal fulfilment is projected above the wearisome urge of cramming junk among others. Mindful consumption is the concept that encompasses the antipodal principles of minimalism, which encourages people to stop and intentionally think about all the purchases they make as well as their worth to them. It also encourages people to develop a high level of consciousness and awareness in regards to the impact of their consuming decisions on themselves, on other people as well as on the planet as a whole. This precious chapter seeks to unveil and take the readers through the principles and practices of mindful consumption and establish how they could create a more personalized and less materialistic world that is also in alignment with one's values and conscience, and that is also much more respectful of the world we inhabit and the technological dystopia it tends to unleash on its inhabitants.

Beyond doubt, consumption is an inseparable thread of the contemporary civilization with people, from the moment of childhood, being overshadowed with the messages that advise them on how to equate their self-identity or self-worth with the products they own. Advertising, social media, and culturally imposed ideals; these messages all strongly back the belief that the acquisition of wealth in the form of goods and property was the only measure of success, happiness, and personal liberation. Many people, thus, think that the more things they own, the more fulfilled and happy they would be. Nevertheless, this attitude fosters an insatiable and perpetual cycle of consuming or excess as well as changes in lifestyle that have a negative effect not only on the consumers' well-being but on the community and the global ecology as well. Particularly, mindless consumption leads to the incapacity to overcome a dilemma of better products and polished resources until the change is irreversible, which, in turn, causes incessant environmental issues as well as overwhelming waste. Besides, it encourages a feeling of discontent, as the chase for possessions and wealth is grounded in the belief that finally owning the desired item will bring the next level of happiness when in essence it seldom does, leaving however newly frustrated, full of anxiety, and detached from other people and purpose in life.

Mindful consumption challenges this all-the-more-tellable paradigm by advocating for an even more deliberate and thoughtful approach to how we consume. It tries to make us consider the real value of the things we buy and use, inviting us to prioritize quality over quantity wanted as sustainability over convenience, and caring more about experiences than possessions. By engaging our focus from acquiring more to living more intentionally, we can genuinely break free from the cycle of consumerism and create a life that is much richer in meaning, purpose, and connection; now, we have the propensity of making our lives freer from the dragging choices that come with unmindfulness in consumption.

One of the immediate principles of mindful consumption is that of intentional purchasing. In a world where shopping has become an unusual common pastime, and impulse buying is often encouraged, this intentional purchasing forcefully requires us to slow down and carefully consider each purchase before making it. This calls for even asking ourselves whether the item we are considering truly does add any value to our lives, whether it aligns with our values and goals for human existence, and whether it is something we genuinely require in the human existence at that moment or even want in the moment. Adopting such a mentality, we can easily avoid the pitfalls sometimes made due to impulsive buying which subsequently reduces the clutter that often accumulates in our homes and minds; also going for such a meaningful kind of conscientious buying could make us use our resources in an intelligent way and act as though they really are valuable instead of treating them as some frivolities in our lives.

But furthermore, intentional purchasing does involve being mindful of the broader impact that our consumption choices and trends have on the world around us. Every one product we buy has a whole life cycle that goes beyond our immediate use in the job market, from the extraction of raw materials through long and intensive production and possibly laborious and costly transportation until they finally arrive at the market, and straightforward and unceremonious disposal. This particular life cycle has substantial and progressive environmental and social implications, such as concerning carbon emissions and generally pollution, problems related to waste through all its explorable dimensions, and issues potentially arising from working labor practices in various countries. By considering these vast factors in our purchasing decisions, we can make ethical and sustainable choices, thus supporting companies and products that align with our values, and finally contributing to the greater good as well as enhancing the whole value of our existing exchanges in this world.

Consumerism represents a range of intertwined issues in modern society, making it essential to practice sustainable consumption. Minimalism is a philosophy that encourages simplification and minimization but promotes an environmentally friendly lifestyle such as_, which encouraged conscious purchasing, desiring only to purchase what is important, or what adds value to life thus leading to responsible and ethical consumption habits_ By buying fewer things, we, in effect produce fewer products which again put pressure on the environment through the extraction of natural resources and degradation locally and globally. We can consume by making sure to choose those products with the least adverse environmental impacts, like those made from biodegradable raw materials, manufactured locally to support the local economy, durable, and repairable. It is also conscious consumerism through which we can choose to support only those companies whose practices are ethical and socially responsible with regard to their employees, the environment, and transparency in their operations. Eco-friendly consumption involves a shift in our thinking from just viewing consumption as a cycle of making the right choices to realizing the connectedness of our combined actions with the environment, that each tiny activity influences elaborate systems filtering through our world.

Another outstanding factor is that a reduction of waste offers another approach of unhealthy consumption patterns and mindful consumption. In a society where Instead of using environmentally friendly items that only serve a single purpose, it is important for all the consumers to opt for methods that will help reduce the levels of waste created. Many conscious efforts can be made by shoppers such as buying things in large quantities so as to cut packages, composting organic waste, and using reusable items such as bags and containers instead of one-time use items such as packs and carrier bags. The thing is again that it involves a little focused thinking to repair an item when it is spoilt rather than throwing it away or redistributing items that are not needed by us but can still be used for some other cause. Instead of merely being environmentally conscious, minimizing waste is about developing an attitude of ability and originality, about taking satisfaction in maximizing what we possess on an everyday basis instead of merely have new products. In making all responsible and positive decisions, the additional result is that we tend to experience various new sides of life that we never thought that could be fun. Significantly, the approaches discussed above act to improve current patterns of relating to material things in the new society. However, this does not mean that one has to be perfect in order to make a change. begin with the little chances and begin to integrate more and more of these principles in your life- arise from underneath and make a difference. It is through being more mindful in our consumer behaviors; that we can provoke transformations that will lead this world towards a better living environment for all.

The philosophy of being thoughtful in terms of consumption of things and living our lives is associated with the idea of giving more importance to the quality of the thing instead of the quantity of the thing. In a society that constantly encourages people to be lavish and extravagant, choosing to live a life that is about having only a few things that are of the highest possible quality is a truly strong form of communication. Quality over quantity means to purchase and own well crafted, functional products that would last for years to come even if the outlay for this initial purchase is more. This move not only helps to reduce the trash we produce as consumers and the junk we eventually send to landfills but also helps to save a considerable amount of money as far as consumers are concerned in the long-term. In addition to all this, it helps to deepen our relationship with what we own since looking after and making the most out of what we choose to own means to cherish what you own and have. Because we only buy and look after things that we are really emotionally connected and invested in the desire to replace or upgrade items in a short amount of time is diminished. This practice does not stop at material possessions; it reaches out to all the spheres of the life where it propounds that we dedicate our lives to pursuing actual value and quality, in lieu of the superficial experiences, dissatisfied commitments, and empty engagements.

Today, as we mold in the fast-paced digital age and technological advancements of digital media, being an intentional consumer has to extend beyond the basic principles of consumption as discussed above to the type of consumption that we have with the digital products as well as services proclaimed above. The overwhelming availability of content, the lure of digital convenience, and the environmental impact of digital technologies together present some formidable obstacles to the practice of living a minimalist lifestyle. The purchase of hardware for digital consumption, the reduction of time spent in front of screens, and the consideration of the consequences for the environment in the online environment, the issue of digital consumption is a relevant theme. Mindful digital consumption means going about things with a sense of discrimination, making sure that the content we consume adds value to our lives rather than contributing to the sensory overload and distractions we already encounter. At the same time, human beings are creatures made for relationships, and this means that connection and immersion in the world of real experiences are things that our souls and hearts crave and desire. Therefore, it boils down to creating and keeping a balance between the advantages and benefits of the digital realm and the necessity to take part in and live the physical world where healthy relationships with people, places, and things one can feel and see become available and real.

The intention to implement a practice of mindful consumption is not solely confined to the need for following harsh rules or enduring hardship in materialistic requirements. In contrast to this, it is making selections that are governed by the principle of aptitude and that add to leading a satisfied and meaningful life that can be likened to a sauce of happiness. It is about an innate realization that our existential value does not rest on the immense possessions rather it is established on the quality of our general conduct. Also known as mindful consumption, this consumption clears space within the self as well as the outside world of the consumer for matters as well as items of real significance. The act of being in sync with one's requirements and wishes as well as establishing more substantial hereditary ties with one's surroundings, fellow beings and the earth are possible in a spirit of harmony. People can center their lives more and more in a positive way and act with intention in a purposeful manner by consuming in a conscious manner that develops awareness and reach to delve deeper into themselves.

This current chapter seeks to investigate how people can be mindful consumers in every aspect of their everyday lives and as such offering useful insights and actionable tips that teach one on how to be more deliberate in their choices about things. Whether it is crucial purchasing decisions, minimizing waste production, employing better sustainable practices, or digital minimalism, the principles that will be put across in this chapter lay down a guide on living in a manner that is both responsible and personally fulfilling. The truth is that mindful consumption is a mantra and a challenging method of being and living in this world as a way of careful conduct and action that acknowledges the interconnections of all beings. In addition, this way of ethical consequences tends to note the necessity of impacting positively on the environment in which we live and to which we belong and to respect the well-being of other human beings.

In the practice of mindful consumption, we are called to walk out of the treadmill of constant acquisition and into a zone of respectfulness and contentment for what we have. It is in this approach that we learn to fully understand the idea of simplicity and experience the feeling of joy that comes with a better understanding and appreciation for simple things. The fact is that life can be so confusing, with a multitude of filtering through situations, a specific mass of things, and a volume of unilinear lives being so difficult to focus on. As we implement and thrive in this kind of lifestyle, what we finally get to discover is that real wealth is not about accumulating items, but about enhancing a well-lived life that is characterized by purpose, connections, and appreciation. Mindful consumption is a tool that has the potential of leading to better impacts on the environment in which we live and to which we belong while at the same time being transformative and growth-provoking as it allows one to become in touch with the very vital aspects of ourselves in a way that nourishes our deepest and most authentic selves.

The Art of Intentional Purchasing

In a massive world of consumption where buying has become the order of the day, the idea of intentional buying provides an antithesis in the way we buy the products and services we need. Central to this practice is the persistence on making careful and conscious decisions any purchases are made on the basis of one's values, needs, and long-term goals instead of by emotion, peer pressure, or temporary desires. The foundation of minimalism with its focus on straightforwardness and intention to live according to principles creates a strong base for living, it helps the people to understand the real significance of things in one's life and affirms what any individual chooses to bring in their existence as important and valuable.

The society of modern world culture propagates that "the feeling of joy and completeness are things that are achievable through acquisition of a lot of things" while stating that acquisition of possessions will surely make one complete in this life. Advertisements, social media, and to an extent the people we closely associate with instil this belief stealing our freedom, and indicating that we are nothing but what we have and spend. Hence numerous "suspects" involved in the vicious circle of consumption that occurs when we continuously spend money on something new expecting it to bring us the excitement or position we want in life. Nevertheless, this approach very often ends to being a cause of unorganized households, unrealistic budgets, and constant emptiness, since the new goods spell the beam of allure for some time and the constant looking forward to the new acquisition cannot make people fulfilled.

In contrast, intentional purchasing provides an opportunity to break this vicious circle of consumption by stopping and deciding before buying. It helps us answer the questions is this really adding value to my life, is this object in accordance with my principles and life objectives, is this something that I really want or something that I want temporarily. Obeying the system of delicate observance in consumption is not about worse living or cutting down on the quantity of purchased products, it is just about making examinations and embracing those items that fit our real beliefs and need as opposed to feelings or acquaintances as the influence from the external world. Intentional purchasing is a way to appreciate one's surroundings and the experience of having products that are significant and that change one's living and lifestyle positively. By consciously and constructively taking charge of what they introduce to their lives, people can develop a sense of satisfaction, happiness, and contentment which would otherwise be impossible to achieve in the competitive life of modern materialistic society. Thus, in a culture that preaches supremacy of consumption as a solution for satisfaction, intentional purchasing can be an avenue for not merely existence but for leading a deliberate, richer, and therefore, more gratifying life.

One of the most efficient and effective tools for becoming an intentional consumer is the act of pausing before buying. This amendment automatically allows a period for concentration within which we can think critically and determine if a potential purchase is actually needed and useful or simply an impulse moderation. During this reflexive interlude, there are certain important questions that we should all put to ourselves: Is this something that I need in my life or is it something that I simply want? Is this purchase going to be something that is going to be of sufficient value that I obtain it, or is it simply a temporary fix to a deeper-rooted desire or emotion? Do I really have to acquire this thing that I want to buy now, and how does it relate to my core beliefs and aspirations? By deliberately considering these simple yet highly critical questions, we are all in a good position to make more informed and sensible decisions which would go a long way in reducing the likelihood of acquiring unnecessary things in life or if so; things we desire but do not actually needs.

Another very crucial aspect of intentional purchasing is weighing the benefits of long-term purchases against the allure of short-term gains and pleasures. Without any iota of doubt, many expenditures are directed towards the desire for immediate satisfaction-a quick boost, pleasure, or relief. But unfortunately, this type of satisfaction is very short-lived and disappears almost immediately, and in the end, one is left with items that seem to lack value and purpose in life. Intentional purchasing is different from this type of behaviour since some people engage in it. It goes beyond instant satisfaction and compels consumers to think as far as the future on the usefulness of a purchase to them. Would this item's continued use, enjoyment, or enhancement of our lives stand the test of time or, on the contrary, will it turn into yet another object of possession? When we place emphasis on long-term gains instead of short-term desires, we are bound to make purchases that are aligned with our inner self and have the potential to contribute positively to our lives.

Stressing the importance of prioritising needs and doing away with wants is the last piece of the useful puzzle of intentional purchasing. In consumer societies that tend to redefine the thin line between real needs and superficial wants, it is often hard to distinguish between and think of the two differently. But the strength of intentional purchasing calls for such distinctions and urges us to meet genuine human needs before indulging our specific needs. This does not imply that we do not have to partake in such exciting and beautiful things out there that come our way. Instead, it means that we consciously treat the act of fulfilling our personal desires instead of going to alter the priority of our bought goods or waste our money. When we outline our basic needs and work with them, we provide ourselves with a sense of stability and tranquillity that allows us to enjoy life and buy things that would enhance and give pleasure to our existence without the basic financial considerations and the false guilt that come with the thought of overconsumption.

Intentional purchasing can be actually as the practice of consciously buying things that will add value to one's life and that one truly needs. It fosters a deeper appreciation for the things we have and obtain. This concept encourages us to think carefully about our purchases and the way we treat such articles. And just because we've developed a better sense of appreciation, we've begun valuing what we have sufficiently, thus reducing the desire to indulge in a cycle of constant acquisition. In addition, through intentional purchasing, we start making choices that are centered on investing in quality over quantity. At times, what we need to purchase are durable products which will last long instead of buying disposable products which never satisfy our needs for long. However, the notion of intentional buying does not just reduce the situation of clutter and excessive spending but also forms a path to sustainable and fulfilling living.

When we talk about intentional purchasing, it is important to note the essence of minimalism. This remarkable technique is often referred to as living with a vision and understanding of what it is that one truly needs. By emphasizing what it is that matters the most and removing what does not, we come up with the space that creates room for all the activities and experiences that can help us grow and become better people. This understanding of the true meaning of life and the purpose of the purchases we make gives us a lot of power in our choices, guiding them with value and the true purpose they are intended for. By doing so, we resist outside forces as well as momentary desires that can lead to bad purchases or even regret. At the same time, it means that we make fewer purchases and make better choices about the things we buy. When we are able to think once again about the eco-friendliness of our products, both in terms of their impact on the environment and their effect on society, it means that the goods that we buy have an independent and responsible production process.

It is also very interesting to consider the psychological benefits of intentional purchases. When we choose deliberately, make thoughtful decisions about what to buy and how to spend in a conscious compelling way, the heart knows there is a difference and this can help lead to a feeling of clenching that is felt right when making the acquisition. This sense of control over one's own life can help deal with stresses when people make impulse purchases without application of reflection or approach. This ability also contributes to a more relaxed and manageable mental condition. Besides that, as anthologized up with trend of minimal living through conscious consumerism, a powerful affirmation of what latently adds integers to one's existence. By following intentional purchasing, it projects a bombardment of positive values fragmenting the very fiction of contentment or lack of appreciation which is the bane of modern-day society. The feeling of gaining satisfaction through simple yet valuable things is what becomes a badly desired haven of true longevity.

Intentional purchasing is a practice that needs to be understood well, with the utmost thought, dedication, and mindfulness. In a world where you see advertisements everywhere, then it is never easy to ignore the cries of consumerism and select between what you truly need and the wants that are pushed by the outside world. However, the upside to practicing the art of intentional shopping is richly rewarding. By making a conscious choice and being selective in the things we purchase, one can, not only live a life that is sustainable and aligned with the values of the individual but a life that is also enriched in meaning and a sense of satisfaction that is hard to explain.

This intentional purchasing is an art that offers just as much as it takes, the space to act and cultivate the sense of intention in one's life on both levels of personal and materialistic levels by clearing the monotony and distraction of consumerism. The process allows the buyer to choose things that reflect his true interests and wishes, to recognize the worth of the things he accepts in his life, and how to make an informed, intricate, and genuine acknowledgment of those things. It is through this utilization of the purchasing capability with full awareness that not only does intentional buying become a useful exercise, but also a path to living conscious, prosperous lives. Thus, intentional purchasing innovative practices that can positively alter the course of our time on earth and the lives we breathe into our relationships, the environment, and our states of being.

The Harmony of Simplicity and Sustainability

The term minimalism denotes the advisory feature of an objective attitude toward the adoption of a minimalist way of life in the present day, where the impact of human activity on the ecology of our planet becomes more and more visible, and the philosophy of minimalism not only helps improve the quality of life of a person but also contributes to the health of our planet. Minimalism, with its concentration on simplicity and building a system of values in life, is a natural ally of the principles of sustainability, calling upon each individual to consume less, be mindful of their choices and attune themselves to the natural necessities of the ecosystem. By accepting a minimalist way of life, we can very gradually start to reduce our ecological footprint, promote realization of ethical principles, and provide a habitability of our planet for the generations to come.

Minimalism and the philosophy of environmental sustainability stress the idea of the less is more. Minimalism at its heart, bibliographically scrutinizes the reigning consumerism ethics that sells the notion of happiness and achievement through the acquisition of material things. This continuous cycle of producing several things together to meet the needs of the masses creates a demand for natural resources that come with an environmental cost. The overexploitation of the earth's natural resources is accompanied by the destruction of natural habitats and certain species of animals become extinct. Partaking in the manufacturing processes may result in considerable pollution of the air and water shed with industrial wastes and production of tons of greenhouse gases while excessive transportation of products spread across the globe leads to transportation emissions thus increasing the carbon footprints of the goods being consumed.

Minimalists who consciously decide not to engage in such practices have the power to reduce the impact on the environment. The topics of reduction and consumption reduction lead directly to the challenges of the extraction of raw materials and depletion of resources, the prevention of the consumption of large amounts of energy in the processing of the products, and the speaking the climate of new products transported over large distances. In this way, minimalism has direct relevance to reducing the environmental impact of human activities and thus contributing to diminishing the carbon footprints of individuals. Furthermore, in selecting the quality of items rather than their quantity, the supporters of minimalism tend to purchase old, durable, product items with a long lifespan, which in turn reduces the everyday need for product refills as well as their adherence to the environmental costs.

Minimalism is a approach that many people are inclined to pursue that inspires people to embrace the principles of sustainable living in the most honest of ways. These changes begin at the level of the lifestyle choices that minimalists make in the products they buy and the companies they choose to buy them from. This way of thinking and acting creates awareness, that is one of the things that sets minimalists apart from regular buyers. For example, minimalists tend to go for the products that do not affect the environment much, for instance, products made from renewable or recyclable materials or products produced through sustainable methods. They get products that are designed to be more energy-efficient or to have a smaller environmental impact in production. By putting their money towards purchasing such items, minimalists not only help in reducing their environmental impact as individuals but also have part in the creation of a quot;green economy" by supporting the companies committed to eco-friendly practices and with environmentally conscious values.

This consumer activism can be seen in a way, as a model for embracing the ethical approach of modern consumers also and making companies with the same understanding know that people are most interested in supporting them. Many minimalists make the conscious choice of sourcing their goods from companies that are known for their Ethical Code of Conduct and for upholding not only sound environmental ethical practices but also sound protection of the rights of workers. Such businesses are known for sourcing from suppliers that treat workers fairly and with respect and that put the welfare of the people and the environment first. For example Flower Child can as businesses go above and beyond and State Chest that Rather than undermining the usage of products that are made cheaply or Torre that is the production of people will not even sympathize with minimalists. By being but as a choice on purposely and supporting these businesses, minimalists are in fact proving that they can send a message with their cash that is a strong as any other and that is hence the beginning of a trend for businesses to be sustainable and deal with their corporate social responsibilities seriously. This is a positive marketing sphere that can be formed when people minimize their minds and consumers take the next step in ensuring that they are treated safely and remodeled and customers are indeed created.

Another important part of the little minimalism in that it helps a person to be very careful on what is used and on the disposable products or Single-use Goods instead of re-purchase as seen above in how little rubbish may be created while still application of the idea of minimalism. Minimalists often take a closer consideration of the number of disposable products people often deal with as part of our everyday lives but are more commonly not being looked at. Some of them are those plastic bags that people use for shopping, plastic water bottles, food packaging, and the like. Disposable products end up in the environmental milieu without proper recycling and adding unsightly things that have not been able to degrade or corrupt for literally hundreds of years. Such type of products are made using materials that cannot be decomposed and that's probably the most negatively impacting aspect about such type of products. Disposables or single-use items have created a lot of plastic and last for a very long time. The excess waste in landfills and the continued toxic pollution of oceans, and the devastating effects of marine life can take a toll which cannot be overemphasized as a result of this practice. Minimalism encourages the use of durable and reusable items to replace disposables and to add to its value. When minimalism people make conscientious choices to get items that are reusable like shopping bags, water bottles, food containers, and other daily usage items among others, they can dramatically decrease the wastefulness of their habit, as well as the negative impact on the environment, created by such habits. The adoption of one person leads to the chain reaction of others adopting it and thus setting an example for others discouraging a throwaway culture

The minimalist approach to reducing waste goes beyond the avoidance of disposable products, with an aim to see everything differently. This is a significant aspect that squarely revolves around how to master resourcefulness and conservation. Minimalists are not the quintessential proponents of waste; they have made it a habit, and it has encapsulated their beliefs and other lifestyle choices, by repairing what they can instead of replacing them, buying pre-loved or upcycled products that prevent stress on the already burdened earth, and even thinking outside the box while it comes to repurposing or reusing those old and worn-out items that have been left lying around for years. By employing these ingenious techniques to our possessions, which are done through an invaluable and subjective lens, it is possible to not only reduce waste but also come to appreciate the true value of everything that we possess, which cannot be matched with the realities of a throwaway culture that is every so often liberated in the entry of modern society.

Consequently, while minimalism is commonly considered a personal strategy to improve one's well-being—ideals such as reducing stress and anxiousness, increasing concentration and efficiency, and being more satisfied with the life we lead—it is also important to see that the benefits of minimalism go beyond the personal. By taking a conscious decision to consume less, purchase from ethical suppliers, and reduce waste, what minimalists do is not just about bettering themselves but rather they are helping to heal and sustain the earth for future generations. By embracing such a view, we cannot help but notice that everything on this planet is interlinked and the choices we make every day have far-reaching impacts all over the globe. This ought to be understood; furthermore, minimalism requires that we understand that the well-being of the whole planet calls for the entire human race to act as a single organism.

Minimalism, as a philosophy, is neither about depriving ourselves of what we love nor living only with bare essentials. It is about being conscious of our beliefs and aspirations, about living a life of purpose and intention in every area of our lives, and addressing the sustainability of our lifestyles. What minimalists do is attempt to skip the junk of over-consumption and ride into the glorious beauty and richness of a true life. The approach opens up its understanding to consumption with the sense that the Only Sufficient Available World exists as an acknowledgement of our feeble place within this magnificent realm which is frequently unstable. Wearing minimalism in mind directs the thought and urges us to live in a way that respects our environment and tries to reduce the negative impact that our actions have on it. By implementing fundamental techniques of minimalism not only do we reduce the negative effects witnessed over the environment but we do also enhance our own psychological and physical wellness and therefore create a resoundingly bright world possible for the generations to come.

The synergy between minimalism and sustainability is not just triaged to decreasing environmental footprint, rather it has to do with a deepened sense of connection with our surrounding environment. As we start simplifying our living, forgoing materialistic occupations, and honing activities that tend to matter in real sense, we become more in tune with the natural phenomena of life, sense the varied wonders of nature, and see the provision of nature as in plenty. This equation does not only help us in individually creating these connections but also nudges us into ascending collectively to live entitled in unison with nature provided we can attest that our personal aspirations are closely knit with the well-being of the earth by enhancing this compact mutually.

Additionally, by instilling a minimalist approach in our lives, we commence a chain effect of motivation towards others to do the same. The decisions we render and support--be it consuming less, adopting sustainable measures, or cutting down on personal waste--are capable, in some measure, to exercise influence on our colleagues and friends, thus being constituents in a wider mode-shifting towards sustainability. From this point of view, minimalism essentially becomes a forceful form of influence for good not merely for the individuals implementing it but also for the entire population into the world.

Thus, it can be concluded that the integration of minimalism and environmentally friendly living is a unique composition, where both ideas mutually nourish and support each other. By minimizing consumption choices, making decisions with care, and minimizing waste, minimalists are well-placed to create a palpable reduction in their carbon footprint as well as sustain the globe. Living this way, it may be stated, does not only prize an individual but also caters for a bigger angle of taking care of nature and to subsequent generations. Minimalism overstated leads us to a more purposeful and intentional way of life that qualifies as a life, which is not only simpler and gratifying but also lies in a notion of supporting our responsibilities, to our values in caring and revering our environment and our place as its caretakers. The confluence of sparseness and sustainability generates an impact, which can make a great deal of good in a multi-faceted society, epitomizing a pathway to an optimistic and profoundly sustainable future for the world.

The Art of Living with Less Waste

Finding a suitable balance between powered devices and the natural surroundings is petroleum-consuming thing for a use and throw society. In such a debate, generating less trash is a huge relevance since it is a better way to imply devoted attention to the house we inhabit- Mother Earth. Naturally, the interesting goal of reducing waste is much attuned to the core notion of minimalism, which appears to be a more focused, realistic living. When there was a regular practice of reducing the waste that we produce, we are not only contributing positively to our environment but achieving a sense of joy, contentment, and satisfaction in our everyday lives. This practice thus basically comprises philosophical principles, thus saying that materialism and excess chomping into our lifestyles honor the delicate nature of our planet as well as realize how our choices, from the simplest to the hardest tasks of life, affect the different lives thereof in the planet.

And now we come to the significant platform of strategies that reduce the amount of waste emanating through the of reducing, reusing, and recycling. Whenever these rules are put into practice, we can reduce the ways in which we may impact the environment by a wider margin, through which we may develop more of an appreciation of the rich biodiversity of our planet. Each of the three R's outlined carries with it that specific alteration of point of reference from the ingrained shrugging approach to the disposal that is deeply ingrained in the culture of wastefulness that speeds up environmental hazards, to a perspective that is more deeply ingrained in the ecology that is much slower and considers the relationship of environment and man with each other and the effects of earth at present and the future.

In order to regard a grain of sand as the basis for a building, more roguelike things should be addressed than were then anticipate, out of which is the phenomenon of minimalism as movement as part of the 'R's, basically talking about buying less. Numbers say that, when it comes to the out of an enormous amount of waste, it is integrally nothing. By only purchasing what really matter to us, for example, which generates no overspending for the again emphasizes the point of good over the Volume, we might a lot of rubbish. Do not actually consider the product's entire flow from the cradle, its production, and all the subsequent throw-offs that go into production. And, it goes without saying, to avoid any items that could be used only once, hoarded due to some other insignificant factor, or are the source of the problem of ever-increasing plastic use. Because when we buy less, we not only lower the desire for sectoral production and formation but also scale down waste caused due to packaging, hence, decaying the leather finally. Purchasing a 2 liter soft drink bottle of Tarzan from a gas station and throwing it into a trash bag as you are washing out of your car might not seem like a big deal, however the immediate impact that those activities have is devastating and at times unknown in a globalized economy in which what seems to be innocuous may contribute to a dreadful decline to hamper life on our planet.

One practical way that we can reduce a significant amount of waste in our daily life is really by looking to buy products in bulk. By looking at bulk purchasing, one is able to minimize waste regarding packages as it means the figures are not required for items with packages for individual wrapping. Apart from that, it is worth noting that most of the bulk stores provide an option for customers to utilize reusable containers; this is one initiative that also contributes positively towards reducing single-use plastic containers and other package materials. By utilizing our own containers, and buying from bulk sources what we basically need, it is evident that we can significantly reduce the amount of waste which we are sending to landfills. This actions could be thought of as small, they can even cumulatively make a huge positive impact on our environment.

Composting is another significant tool recognized in reducing waste where the process focuses on organic materials, which is very crucial. When it comes to food scraps, yard waste plus other organic matter, this could fit a very high portion of the house waste that if left unchecked is sent to landfills, contributing to the production of methane gas given that it is a highly powerful greenhouse gas. The banana-peel or broccoli stem pizza waste we create in our kitchens and gardens can be avoided through composting by turning it into nutrient-rich soil that carries minerals and substances that a garden or a plant can thrive on. This method not only reduces the amount of waste we produce but also promotes a more sustainable, environmentally friendly model where waste is transformed into a resource. This system not only gives us full control over the waste we produce but at the same time, provides for a ready supply of compost for our gardens.

Another important approach that we can employ in realizing a world of less waste is carrying out repairs to items present rather than throwing them away. In that? In a culture that champions throwing things away, some consumers would prefer to replace items that are either broken or worn out instead of repairing them. This practice leads to a buildup of waste, apart from depleting Mother Nature's resources. There is something noble in repairing something that doesn't work, be it a shirt, a radio, or a toaster, at least we are of the view of extending the lifetime of the objects and therefore minimizing the need for raw materials. It encourages us to respect and take care of what we already have, rather than treating them as expendable items which we can choose to replace whenever we want. It passes the practical benefit of extending the life of a product that one loves while Ondas something much deeper presente in the culture of consumption and a throwaway.

When we talk about the numerous benefits that can be achieved by starting to follow a zero-waste way of living, many people think that it is simply about getting rid of all the trash. The truth is that zero to waste is a vision or an ideal for life and it is not about perfectionism or denying the way we consume, but rather about trying to reduce waste as much as possible, using more environmentally friendly alternatives, and choosing wiser options in every little thing that concerns waste streams, from the moment we purchase a product to the way we throw away or fix it. It aims to increase awareness about our waste-output behavior and do what is right for the environment, acknowledge the issues, and stand a chance to combat them, though everybody should realize that an ideal, truly zero-waste lifestyle is not very realizable but always a target which helps people become aware of their habits and consume in a more thoughtful way, creating a better relationship with the world, and generating new skills and practices that can increase their lives and make our planet a better place.

Living a zero-waste life is not just about environmental conservation, but personal well-being. When we look for "true values" and a better style of life including less impact on the environment, we create an incredible sense of accomplishment that comes from living according to "our own convictions" and trying to perform right and make a contribution to the betterment of the environment and the future for the following generations. Reducing waste also means removing the unnecessary physical and emotional burden from our lives, and therefore zero waste easier gets together with the philosophy of minimalism, which is the disrobing of the process of declining things and experiences in life to only things and experiences that mean the most to a person. It is easier to appreciate materially important facets of life and things that bring you satisfaction when the material aspects are eliminated and the focus is shifted to the personal side while the person lives out of the material aspect, not for improvement.

What is more, what's significant about the process of reducing waste is that it actually cuts costs. That is being less consumptive, mending what's broken instead of tossing it, buying products in bulk and not taking unnecessary gadgets and other disposable things, we nullify the wasteful and useless processes as well as save our own money. Not only do these ideas help to relieve or decrease the stresses that are associated with finances, but they also allow one to use the saved funds in a more sensible way for the satisfactions that develop a person and build a social nature of one. The realization of the financial advantages of a zero-waste style of life goes well with the ideas of the philosophy of minimalism that states that purposeful living, and the prioritization of things positively influences the level of satisfaction in life.

Many individuals would attest that waste fast consumption and throwaway culture can cause abuse to our ecosystem as well as disconnect among people. Waste reduction practices like composting, bulk buying and repairing products are often are done within community collaborations or actively engaging some local businesses. Practicing these waste management methods creates and keeps relevant ties between people because through these activities our engagement, networking, sharing of knowledge and skills all help in the direction of continuous progress towards sustainable living just like in the quest for greener lifestyles today. There are a number aspects of living minimally which revolve around building relationships rather than accumulating possessions.

Beginning a journey of living with minimum waste may seem incredible owing to the difficulties this premise would pose. It takes a person who is committed and determined to go against society's standards, make considered behaviors every minute throughout the day. On the other hand, though, there are very many advantages to living that way. Every time we cut on waste production, we are making a chance for our planet but also living a more purposeful life that matches what matters most with our hearts, people we love, and causes, everything else in the world with the deepest values.

By embracing an attitude of living with little waste, we give a strong testimony of the kind of world that we long for—where every resource is respected, every waste is minimized, and the earth plus the future generation is the most important element. This theory of existence delves deeper into the idea of green living because it's about awareness of purpose and discipline and satisfaction in daily living. Going on and learning how to live minimally while producing less waste and practicing minimalism, we can design a life that not only allows us to live environmentally friendly but gives us an opportunity to leave planet Earth with a sense of fulfillment that is so rare.

The Value of Lasting Quality

In the fast-paced world of endless longings and escalated desires for possessions under the intangible allure of "newer is tangibly better", the minimalist theory of adopting "high quality valuing approach rather than high quantity approach" serves the purpose of equally countering these acceptable cultural superficialities. In itself, it would challenge how common people regard the use of consumer items that break easily and how they pile things up in ways that do not add value to them. It proffers an alternative principle prioritizing durable articles with utmost craftsmanship and efficiency that point to a secondary focus on fleeting things, as well as the ethical acknowledgement for perpetuating harmful consumerism. By adhering to the idea of "Only Buy Once, Buy Well", we are offered a path that goes beyond excess and wastefulness, implying a more personal commitment towards the things we own as well as adopting a different way of living, one that is conscious and correct.

At the very foundation of "Quality over Quantity" is the meaningful conception which captures the idea that not everything that is marketed and known as a consumer good is of the same quality. A mass-produced article might serve specific purposes, however depending on its cost and low prices, there is no commitment to high standards of durability, strength, or level of satisfaction that will keep them loyal for many years to come. That is to say even if they appear as cheaper options, these relatively cheaper articles invariably become disposable, thus even further polluting the environment by landing constantly at our dumpsites thus inviting another cycle of consuming. On the other hand, high-quality objects, while their initial price tag may be substantially higher, function on a different wavelength. Such objects are manufactured following laborious methods and with superior materials that should hook consumers; the assumption to stick to what is good for the world, consumers should not give up on the manufacturers for these products. With these durable items, however, consumers have the privilege of saying no to a replacement chip, embrace, and appreciate the value of goods, realize its satisfaction in an array of years and even pace longer.

Purchasing high-quality goods is not simply a matter of either edging an unconsidered effort or squandering more money but a kind of choice to ponder carefully in regard to what specifically is most susceptible to staying true in an environment that constantly prompts people to consider quick fixes, surface-level plasticity, or cheapness. Countless findings show how immediately out of mindset poise is a powerful catalyst to instill within the minimalist ideology that inspires people to look deeper into what is needed for the world, establishing and putting resources into the things that matter for not only the construction of their present lives but also for future generations. Placing quality before quantity is not solely a matter of consumer choices; it implicitly expresses a creed that protects significance, efficacy, and perpetuity, firmly against transitory pleasures. These intelligent consumers reveal to themselves, to the society, and to the world that true satisfaction and happiness can be achieved by comprehending the on-going earth rather than the barren mind-consuming state already existing whereby ever acquiring more does not contribute to having or being more.

Investing in quality rather than quantity is a principle that when pursued has far-reaching long-term savings that are irresistible. Although the initial price of an item that is of high quality may be on the higher side, its long lifespan and ruggedness mean that it will need replacement less frequently than its cheap counterpart. In this regard, the total cost of ownership is reduced, as is the environmental effect that comes from the manufacturing, transportation, and disposal of many items that are of poor quality. In this manner, it becomes apparent that investing in high-quality products is a financial-wise decision and one that mirrors concern for the present and future environment of the world. This aspect is consistent with the key tenet of minimalism, which is that of being intentional and caring for the environment in the manner one lives.

The slogan of "buy once, buy right" succinctly evokes the axiom of quality over quantity in the purchasing of durable and efficiently functional products. This encourages us to take time to research and choose items to buy that would not only be robustally made but products that meet our needs as opposed to those that are just trendy. Unlike giving in to accidents or even the urge to spend beyond our means on goods that come up daily, we focus on discovering items that make the requirements and resonate with our personal ideals and convictions. This kind of consciousness in buying leads to a tighter bond between us and the products we own as we intelligently choose and purchase only those items that truly depict who we are.

This personal attachment to our properties is one of those salient features of minimalism that many people would not understand through and through. If we put our cash into only the best, the act of taking care of these products goes well beyond the machine for the matter of giving and receiving, which work towards the building of durability and craftsmanship. This care and admiration help to develop a behavior model that abhors both radical replacement and timeless upgrades hence making us more contented people who appreciate the little things in life. Indeed, the option of quality over quantity not only increases personal satisfaction level and happiness but also promotes a sustainable way of life.

We live in a society that often prioritizes the accumulation of material possessions, but the case for or the benefits of prioritising quality over quantity extends far beyond the consumption of physical goods. It is rather a principle that can be applied to all areas of life be it our interpersonal relationships, the work we do, the experiences we have or the meanings we derive from them. Just as we do not want to waste our hard-earned money on shoddy and flimsy items, we must also learn to invest our time and energy in activities and relationships that add value to our lives and are profound. The quality over quantity approach recognizes that what matters most is the depth of our experiences, and therefore, encourages us to seek out that depth by going for deeper experiences and connections that enrich our lives in ways that are more meaningful and enduring.

Take relationships as an example, considering the quality versus quantity principle's perspective, this study reminds us that it is better to have a few deep, meaningful connections with others than to live on the surface with many superficial ones. Through staying constant to relationships that are built on a true foundation of mutual respect, trust, and understanding, we create for ourselves a support system that not only makes us better people but can also sustain us through the vicissitudes and changes of life. Like those things, in our work and personal pursuits, choosing the focus of quality means dedicating ourselves to projects and activities that are on a similar wavelength with us in terms of what we truly are or what we believe in rather than spreading ourselves too thin across numerous, less meaningful or indifferent commitments. By embracing the quality through the quantity principle and letting such quality resonate in our relationships, we create opportunities for growth, support, and fulfillment.

The quality principle is at the same time a guarantee of a more intentional way of living, where every choice we make is for a good reason and for its own sake. This intentionality as well as a conscious effort is a core idea of minimalism which advocates stripping away the superfluous to focus on what is most necessary and what matters in one's life. When we apply the principle of quality versus quantity to the way we lead our lives, we make a conscious decision to link our actions to our values thus creating lives that are holistic, real, and sustainable. We do not just acquire things as status symbols, get sucked up in the frenzy of consumerism, or start relationships or jobs without asking in the first place if they provide us with true satisfaction and happiness. Instead, we start putting our value on the things that matter and that make a difference: the relationships with families and friends that we can develop, the work that we can truly dedicate ourselves to, the things that we can experience at an emotionally genuine and spiritually uplifting level, and the values, opinions, and actions of those people that we can take note of. By determining the quality rather than the quantity of our lives, we adopt a new attitude towards living and the ultimate factor that makes a difference.

Moreover, this approach inspires us to take a moment to pause from the high-speed connected universe we live in nowadays where self-indulgence orders a fixation of immediate results at the moment over a lasting sense of contentment. It beckons us to put the brakes on things, to become conscious of the proficiency and wisdom that produced something of impeccable quality, and to relish the happiness of getting few, good things at once instead of getting more of the sub-standard ones. This approach generates a sense of emotional undemandingness and thankfulness, as we learn to acknowledge the brilliance and effectiveness of well-executed things and the closure of life and the social bonds that mean something to us and cannot lastingly be measured in monetary terms.

As we reaffirm the philosophy of prioritizing quality, we are not merely promising to be friends of the earth and its gifts, but we also vow to lead a life that is fully conscious of the major elements. This choice will help individuals live a more organized, less menacing world that is not just excessively complicated by a desire for control and self-expressive needs and wants but is more in line with one's morals and wants that stem from deep-seated beliefs. This is a type of existence that honors strong textures over flashy cover-ups, solid shape over short-lived designs, active job on formed satisfactions, and junk-late patterns of beholding.

The process of choosing quality over quantity is all about the art of self-regulation and conscious decision-making. It asks of us to take a good look and to scrutinize the ways of consumer society, to defy and come out against the temptations of the quick fixes that make life easier and gives one an immediate sense of satisfaction, and to choose deliberately the things or experiences that matter to us. Into the bargain, this process comes across great improvements: an all-encompassing life filled with richness and value aligned with the present world and its needs, where our taking will reverberate beyond the spell of the instant and the fleeting and last for eternity.

It's this forefront that gives quality to our lives and at the same time helps to create balance and fairness in the world throughout the invitation to a genetically manipulated way of getting producers, recipes, and services out of their best. However, this is the essence of the minimalist philosophy: a life devoted to being wise, using things wisely, and showing reverence for the important people, things, and experiences that dwell within our lives. So I wished I might, and became convinced, the purpose of quality matters and astounding life would unfold in the long run eternal bonds for all of us.

Navigating the Digital World with Intention

In our modern society, the notion of consuming goods mindfully has transcended simply referring to physical products. With our increasing dependence on digital technologies, it has become imperative to apply the same principles of mindfulness and careful consideration to our digital consumption that we apply to our consumption of tangible goods. The digital realm allows us unprecedented levels of convenience and access to information, but it also poses challenges unique to itself, such as the excessive quantity of material available on the world wide web, the environmental consequences of our online activities, and the impact of our lifestyle choices. When we talk about mindful consumption in this digital world, we mean this: it is finding that unique balance we can have while using the technologies in a manner that would be in line with our personal beliefs and morals, could add value to our existence, and would avoid or at least minimize the adverse effects on nature and society at large.

The digital world is large and constantly changing while offering a seemingly never-ending supply of content, services, and software that are specifically designed for the purpose of catching and maintaining our focus. The digital environment from social media platforms such as Facebook/Instagram to streaming services like Netflix; from websites designed for ecommerce to cloud storage and data processing services among many others- all of these are consumables. The huge amount of content available online can at times be quite overwhelming, creating an illusion giving birth to a similar type of clutter as many people's physical space does in their own homes. Digital clutter manifests itself in numerous ways, like a bursting at the seams email account; apps on one's smartphone that do absolutely nothing; social network timelines that instead of enriching us, overwhelm and distract us; the influx of programs and movies on Netflix which we will possibly never view because the idea behind 'Next on my list' concept does not seem acceptable for practical purposes.

Realizing how our lives are seemingly flooded by an unending stream of information is one of the basic things that can begin to make us consume content on the Internet mindfully. Digital convenience makes it easy to indulge in patternive behavior where people consume information unconsciously scrolling through feeds, clicking on links, and allowing the clutter from the Internet to build up without considering the consequences it has on their lives. The mindless consumption of content may come along with certain aspects of life that are probably inconvenient and rather unpleasant, which may be characterized by feelings of being overwhelmed, distracted, and miserable, which may happen because mastering the flow of information and stresses that attention is under is such a difficult task. Thus, under such conditions, using various forms of digital resources we may indeed feel like they steadily drain us of stillness and inner balance and make us anymore anxious, scatterbrained, and fatigued by the end of the day with nothing productive done at all in fact.

Mindful digital consumption implies that we have to consciously choose which sources of information add value to us and which ones do not. This implies having some degree of clarity about the kind of content we want in our lives as well as how it makes us feel or what it does for our growth. By carefully curating the content that we consume, we can eliminate some of the excesses found in today's media, find joy in simplicity, and maintain only those who truly bring value and inspiration to our lives. This intentional approach results not only in less digital clutter in our lives but also in a more intentional approach to our consumption of content and information transferring the power back to ourselves as well." By designing our digital environments mindfully, we can create spaces that reflect who we are truly and support us as we strive towards personal and societal goals that matter to us.

Another critical strategy for mindful digital consumption involves being proactive rather than reactive in engaging with technology and media. This means setting aside time to plan one's online engagement, rather than just mindlessly clicking away at news articles, Facebook posts, or advertisements. For instance, a person can follow certain social media accounts that align with their interests, watch certain YouTube channels focusing on human development and agencies, or maybe join forums where they could find like-minded people. These conscious efforts to follow what they are consuming digitally will help users become more aware of the effects the Internet can have on their lives, be it negative or positive, instead of just letting themselves fall into the trap-not thinking about it and just being carried by the stream. Thus, by being more intentional with our time and focus, we can create an online environment that not only offers the right type of content but also contributes to our growth and the

To counteract the adverse effects of excessive and unintentional digital consumption, it is of the utmost importance that we approach digital consumption with great intentionality. The fact that we can curate our physical spaces in a manner that reflects our values and priorities and thus enhance our well-being can also be applied in our digital spaces that reflect similar criteria in line with our growth in the minimalist principles. The process of culling and editing our digital lives which includes assessing the different apps, subscriptions, media as well as content we engage with on a daily basis with a view to determining if these things truly add value to us is an important aspect of necessary self-improvement with respect to the digital environment we find ourselves in.

The process of curating one's digital library is invaluable and cannot be overlooked if we are going to deal with negative effects of excessive digital consumption. The process of cultivating desired personal capacities and lifestyles in the digital realm follows the same underlying principles as physical decluttering. For instance, one practical way to start the act of separation is to go through an inventory of our smartphone's application files to delete those applications which do not have a well-defined purpose or which have not been used in the recent past. In relation to this, we need to review subscriptions associated with services, software or items such as newsletters in order to cancel the ones that have regularly failed to serve a meaningful purpose in our pursuits. The above actions can help a lot in fine-tuning our technology interactions and establishing a technology culture that is meaningful and focuses on the important things.

Reducing screen time is yet another significant factor to consider when dealing with the issues caused by excessive digital consumption. The advantages of technology cannot be disputed, and its revolutionary tools and practices have transformed how we lead our lives. Unfortunately, the downside is that excessive screen time can lead to a number of adverse effects, such as eye strain, disrupted sleep or poor productivity which tarnish the beauty of technology. What's more, spending too much time looking at screens takes away from precious time that could have been used for performing vital activities such as exercising, reading or even spending time with family. In order to regulate our use of screens, we need to set boundaries and consciously consider the way technology fits into our lives so as we may intentionally supplement beneficial patterns for behavior. This could include setting aside specific periods during which one chooses not to engage in technology whatsoever or having spaces that are devoid of technology as a way of enhancing quality interaction. This kind of practice provides some sort of empowerment as it enables one to break free from mindless screen time and lead a life that is more in sync with what he/she wants to achieve in life.

In this era of advanced digital technologies and rapid developments with a click of a button, environmental sustainability is also an important consideration associated with our digital usage. Although new technologies are recognized for their environmentally friendly nature compared with earlier alternatives, their concentration on physical goods, the world of digital networking, and its components have their own energy footprint too. For instance, the giant servers in data centers demand loads of energy to store and process data while generating immense volumes of scrap. For instance, watching a video online or downloading a large file or saving things in cloud storage consumes a lot of energy, and more than 80% of this energy is still produced from the burning of fossil fuels.

It is our responsibility, as users and maybe even developers of digital technology, to do our best to limit the adverse effect that high-speed technology has on the environment. By being a little more selective and smarter about our digital behavior, it can be possible if we agree on specific strategies to limit our usage. One useful strategy is to lower the resolution of video content or limit the size of files to cut on data usage. Moreover, by being conscious about the reliability of digital information, we can also promote organizations across web-based platforms to address energy issues responsibly in their Data Center operations. Consumers can also choose to support companies that make use of renewable energy sources in their operations or provide users with documented commitments to the environment It may be helpful to reduce usage of some digital services when it is reasonable to do so; this can be illustrated with buying physical copies of books and magazines instead of downloading their e-versions or to participate in numerous meaningful offline activities instead of the presence of the gadget.

We can only achieve a future that is focused on receiving all the advantages of modern technology while also caring for the planet if we realize that there is a need for some fundamental changes. We can argue that we are not being asked to completely abandon doing things in a certain way but instead be smart about the technology we have examined to enhance our lives but not to be overwhelmed or harmed unnecessarily. Changing our digital consumption approaches is influenced by the environmental effects of our choices. Additionally, it enables us to continue enjoying the good things that are present in the world of technology, to use gadgets conforming to modern requirements for life improvement and to opt to harmonize with the modern environment and probably the world. Keeping a sustainable approach towards the world of fast and ever-changing technology is a must as we get used to updating social networks and downloading films clicking away without failure. However, incorporating a mindfully measured approach can be the path towards realizing the most significant aim of the modern society, which is to incorporate the availability of technology with the feeling of the conservation of a planet.

Chapter 6

Minimalism and Relationships

Many people talk about minimalism and they think it is simply about creating minimal spaces with simple living. However, minimalism is deeply rooted in every activity we do. This even includes how we treat our relationships with others in our lives. In these contemporary times, social norms support that having many relationships in your life and being associated with many people is synonymous with being socially successful. However, minimalism offers an interesting twist to this rather unhealthy notion. This philosophy promotes the idea of having wholesome relationships where the focus is more on the quality of the interactions as opposed to quantity or any external appearances. This chapter is about learning how if embraced, minimalism can help us create wholesome relações that truly reflect our authentic selves. It will provide insightful knowledge on how to reduce on the number of people we are friends with but improve on the quality of friendships.

The modernization that has happened all across the globe has led to the formulation of time-consuming and demanding schedules, thus making it difficult for many people to have authentic relationships. Think about the way forwards in terms of new acquaintances, people's profiles on Facebook, and regular conversations on the job, then it is enough to say that a person is bombarded with the great quantity of the social circle the current society requires of him or her. Under these conditions, we may lose sight of those people who matter most to us, these are the family members, and dear ones, or maybe those who believe in us and those with whom we are in a romantic relationship. The idea of the" Minimalism in our relationships" forces us to stop and think about the sphere of our social lives and ask ourselves a series of hard questions on which relationships can be said to have added value to us and which are burdensome to us as people.

 Minimalism in relationships is with the notion of being explicit in our choices. It increases the consciousness about the manner and the persons, with whom we spend the time, showing the discernment to select the people, who positively influence, touch our emotions, and help us to live according to our inner being. The question is not about drawing the line under all our connections and cutting them because we want to apply minimalism in our relationships. Minimalism in relationships encourages us to reveal the facts of life and it shows us another side of friends, in whom we can reconsider the weight on the foundation of intensity based only on intensity. The large number of friends or friends on Facebook does not determine the quality of friendship. It is the choice and the quality of the in-depth connections that are going the way in which they will have a major influence on a person's life. The single selective and essential approach to friendships increases their authenticity and makes them stronger. Using minimalism in these focused, carrying, positive relationships is to remove dirt from our lives, which is why to live with a minimum number of the people who might become a great source of support and fulfillment. With less emotional recollection, we can do more than the quality of our lives, the quality must be improved in particular that we live with people who are going to be very important to us and develop. Failure to use the philosophy of minimalism in; our relationships leads to a life that is full of shallow connections and lacks fulfillment. But by purposefully taking the time that is needed to create stronger and more meaningful relationships, we can achieve a sense of belonging and satisfaction that comes from living an authentic life. Though, with a realization of the fact that minimalism is most certainly a way of life improvements as far as our relationships are concerned, just like I said it is not about getting rid of people who actually matter but entirely working on one one every one at a time, progressive movement which is going to enhance our lives.

Minimalism in relationships is a very important topic. It tips the scale on clearing the emotional clutter from the soul. While we can desaturate our physical backdrop or dwelling place for serenity, in the same sense we can unsaturate the emotional lives that are fruitless and do away with those annoying relationships that have \"outlived their usefulness\" in our existence. These toxic relationships, tat has Noxiousness, manipulation as well as scarcity of reciprocity has been burdensome to bear these, and thus lead us to feel the support of sound self-confidence. In such cases the practices of minimalism persuasion encourage us to keep reviewing these intricate relations and, despite being hard and painful, here separating, distancing, or shutting down certain affiliations that do not add value to our existence is a must. This is important for our overall growth.

However when considering minimalism in relationships, it is not adequate to just some connections, it is also about nurturing the foundations of relationships, the pruning of which leads to improvement in the quality of life. Focusing on quality, we can spend time with fewer people however creating the prosperous bonds of memorable soul mates that are based on unequivocal trust, emotional intimacy, and reciprocation. Being there with a person means that one is willing to converse meaningfully, to expose himself, and flaunt himself with his time yearning for those going through achingly people. It is also a process of illustrating our beliefs about our mode of existence while implanting respect and acceptance in those with whom we are unable to see eye to eye with whether our simplicity as an ideal has been shared or not.

Combining a minimalist mindset in the social realm can be hard especially in an ecosystem that encourages excess and social conformity. Many times you feel the pressure or have been kind but you want to spend time having dinner parties and make every social gathering grand. Nevertheless, that is the lesson from minimalism that as much as the days may be a diehard, we can always keep a meaningful social life and yet carry an empty baggage. While we watch out for the events we participate in and the engagements we make, the people or groups with poor allegiances, we are able to form and maintain social ties of worth without trailing in the quagmire of personal dignity or vulnerabilities the society like scurrying rats at each other.

When it is appropriately applied, the philosophy of minimalism is so powerful that it can enable individuals to build a close relationship and develop trust in their closest relationships. Receiving the visual aspects which consume most of the time and fixing attention on the primary issues with clarity and thoughtfulness helps create appreciative links that are authentically deep for partners, family members, and dear friends. In many occasions, being together or doing things as a couple might not be enough. Equally important is ensuring that one creates a space where credibility and confidences develop over time and where conversations are open and honest while mutual respect exists among family members and friends. A good ground for nourishing trust is laid when this kind of foundation is built since this ensures that the relationships enjoy a blossoming process popularly referred to as growth.

This chapter will outline minimum principles that affect relationships such as how one can stock relationships or throw away emotional baggage. We will also look at the process of demonstrating to our loved ones what we truly believe in while creating time for social interactions but remaining simple in lifestyle choices. Just like a person would probably purchase a few pictures for his house with their favorite colors, minimalism gives an opportunity to have control over one's social life inter-personal relationships in a meaningful way that is bigger than status or material things. In all these discussions, minimalism becomes more than an aesthetic practice as it enhances our connections to those around us on a deeper level. As we pass over into this chapter on minimum relationships, may use intentionality and really make rich relationship experiences that are more voluntary and satisfying, being freed from the bondage of redundancy or disconnection.

The Power of Focused Connections

In today's society, where it often seems as if the number of social connections that one has is a gauge of success, the minimalist approach offers an alternative one that gives more emphasis on the depth and quality of our relationships as opposed to their number. At its emanation, minimalism is simply the act of getting rid of the unnecessary so as to concentrate on that which matters most. When this principle is applied in our social life, it causes people to make connections with others that are likely to be more satisfactory and meaningful, thus making them more likely to last longer. By being anchored at a particular time by the activities that we do and the manner in which we spend our time, it is possible to be in a better position to forge relationships that reflect our inner person. It is through this that we can be able to nurture relationships that boost and fulfill us as well as relationship that enhances us as persons and brings positivity in our lives.

The exceedingly fast pace of life that is the order of the day in the modern world makes it very tricky to have genuine and valuable interaction. In this era of information overload, multiple notifications, and social media pressures to keep in touch with a wide circle of friends, it is indeed easy to be swept away and find ourselves being preoccupied with not everything that matters. In other words, minimalism gives a call to act and think critically about the kind of social life that we lead and the relationships that we attach importance to. It proposes a shift of focus onto significant relationships in our lives which are the most treasured and can be considered as the most want in the present World. These are the people, who support us during hard times, who motivate us to overcome the most devastating challenges in life, and who help us develop and become better human beings.

One critical aspect of living a minimalist life is the idea of "social decluttering." Just as clutter is often removed in the processes of decluttering in our homes to make the environment a better one, it is equally important to declutter our social lives by being more deliberate about the close relationships that we hold dear. Social decluttering does not imply being in a situation where one becomes isolationist and thus distanced from the rest of the society. Rather, it is a more deliberate process of determining where one puts in effort in terms of associations and also where such effort should not be put. One can lessen the number of associations engaged in creating deeper bonds and friendships by letting us put emphasis on the associations and friendships that we hold dear. These are friendships based on fidelity, encouragement, and sincerity that create highly fulfilling recipients of social support.

In the hectic and fast-paced world of today, it is essential to remember just how vital these not only social networks links but real life interactions can make our lives in a way of having meaningful relationships that cannot simply be replaced by quantity. Hence, if you decide to devote time or energy only for specific and valuable interactions with those people around you, it leads to the higher productivity and emotional stability of individuals, as well as, the possibility of feeling better connected with those around us. In short, this step opens a path to a decent and valuable life. When one gives a priority to quality rather than quantity, they can engage with their family and friends so respectfully and as well, attentively that our relationships become deeper and richer.

However, when one is actively at risk of becoming exhausted while trying to look after too many OR numerous ties it becomes much easy to overlook and underappreciate these unique times with dear ones. It is quite easy to look after people in such a manner or become a social zombie but if each one is seen and affects meaningful dialogues instead, these are just another effort at maintaining relationships. Dedicating time is one of the best forms of love and how to speak with the loved ones is even more essentials. Of course, trust and close bonding are necessary components in constructing a strong relationship pyramid but these pillars, in some way, are born and nurtured most simply in these minute intervals of unity or togetherness.

More specifically, through sharing unique moments with them, and laughing and crying with friends or family when changes happen on the table to eat or share with everyone in a dinner, walk, or sit idly, these episodes make the relation or the bond even stronger. Such types of satisfaction offer a few moments of being in quietness and being in peace with the environment that underlines the need for having family and peer support and eliminates the feeling of helplessness in the modern world. This task is another one of Minimalism's many benevolences and it does everything to support the very fact that communities are powerful in our lives. Certainly, Minimalism does not stop with cutting down the number of people in one's life but just as valuable is the fact that's in the effort undertaken to develop healthy, loving, meaningful bonds with people and invest in them.

The Importance of Meaningful Conversations Yet the need beyond these established practices is for genuine, full-bodied exchanges within these meaningful bonds that take active participation. In the digital sphere we now prefer messages as means of communication for instance, so our friends or family members are never taken for granted although this type of communication is often forgettable and frequent. But the crucial benefit of using the Minimalism method and combining quality and short span is that it still gives possibilities for making complex conversations face to face. Such face-to-face meetings should be open such that if on the way a common subject is appraised, facts that were oral and experiences were or a piece of each other's state or feelings were talked about, a window of dialogue and connection between two people is created.

This dialogical model does make it easier for people to build humane and long-lasting relations which are much needed for this fast-moving world. Additionally, by conducting each of these conversations with one's whole attention it is feasible to aim at becoming very clear about what is communicated to one's partner hence creating a powerful mode of an efficient rather than just a verbal exchange. This is not theoretically a part of Humanistic psychology's know-how but it is definitely needed and a bit known practice for those who wish to deepen human relationships.

To summarize, Minimalism enables exactly that: focusing on quantity, fulfilling and real moments means being aware of one's priorities and creating unity and community and meaningful conversations with those important to oneself. It definitely results in completing the empty parts of life and the sense of fulfillment and happiness while it gives respite from constant anxiety and conformity of the world. If in this day and age you feel deprived and isolated when surrounded by many people, try nourishing your quality relationships with only a few Automatically.A goal in itself in friendship and a meaningful link transforms life and attains its sense. Follow the modality that the more important people you actually meet time and internalize due to the right indigenous issues or people, hence&rsquo

Being truly present in our relationships and interactions is not solely about physical presence, but it also refers to emotional and mental connection. It encompasses the ability to suspend all distractions that might interfere with those conversations, e.g., phones or to-do lists, and to dedicate wholly ourselves to the person in question. It is being able to actively listen to the speaker with an open mind and open heart and respond in an understanding and considerate manner. This unique level of presence requires a high degree of practice and commitment to pursuing, yet it is significant in creating and nurturing genuine connections with others. By being totally there for others, we impart a sense of belonging and worth to those around us; thus, establishing an atmosphere in which deep-seated ties are formed. It is in such moments that bonds and attachments are cultivated in an authentic manner by exhibiting a great level of commitment towards the people we consider significant.

Minimalism, the practice of intentionally embracing simplicity, plays a crucial role in enabling the presence of empathy and understanding in relationships with others. As we focus on our lives, removing clutter here and there, and looking around less and less, we can be aware of the needs or feelings of those people in our midst who may need to be encouraged or comforted. We enable ourselves to cultivate a higher degree of emotional availability for others, allowing ourselves to dive into the swimming pool of other people's experiences and feelings with them. This level of empathy is what builds strong connections between us and those people we love the most, as it facilitates in-depth knowledge of who they are, their desires, and how to be present for them. When we approach our social networks with compassion and empathy, we create a bond of mutual faith, understanding, and love that can withstand the hurdles or hardships life throws at us.

Another vital aspect of minimalism is how it enables us to organize the people in our lives based on our beliefs and core values. When we are focusing on what really matters or what is exemplified by our vision, it is natural that we draw people near whom we hold dear and value what we value and those who also aspire to work hard towards these goals. These values create a sense of understanding between us, thus making our relationships a fulfilling and harmonious sphere in which any conflict is minimized. By deliberately bringing important people who encourage and challenge us in the very best ways, we create a community or in essence a family that multiplies our accomplishments and has a full purpose for us as individuals. Therefore, minimalism is a vessel through which we can, create and sustain our most significant and gratifying relationships by being present, compassionate, and aligning our participation in the relationships that matter the most with our core values.

Minimalism in relationships sounds counterintuitive, but it actually offers a fresh perspective on forging genuine connections. Rather than stressing over maintaining a vast network of social media contacts with whom you barely exchange pleasantries, one can concentrate on nurturing the most cherished bonds. Apprehending this fundamental alteration imparts us with the ability to have more fulfilling interactions on this earth and have that joy of connection with our fellow human beings. By establishing relationships that truly resonate with people on a deeper level, we move towards a life enriched by these interactions, one that is honest about its intentions, and is the right thing to do. As a result, we can devote more quality time to what means the most to us in life and what we esteem the most despite the hectic pace of contemporary times.

However, the minimalist perspective regularly has the potential to be a misfit in the modern digitalized world of relationship where more emphasis is placed on the quantity of relations than their quality. By taking charge of our lives and concentrating our time and energy on a small number of select relationships, we can develop deep emotional bonds that meet our needs and give us the sense of belonging that everyone longs for. Building these relations does not entail ordinary chats or possibly small occurrences but rather full-fledged interactions that lead to an experience with other people that feels genuine and alive. Such associations do not merely lift people's spirits or help them fulfil their demands but become reliable rocks in these trying modern conditions as well as provide people with inward health and a sense of stability. The simplicity can develop rich affiliations, which through their care, understanding, and devotion, remedy brokenness and isolation, making the world more connected, filled with sincere feelings, and joyful.

Releasing the Weight of Emotional Clutter

In the practice of minimalism, much attention is often given to the physical act of decluttering—sorting through possessions, deciding what to keep, and letting go of what no longer serves us. Yet, the minimalist philosophy extends far beyond our physical environment. One of the most profound and transformative aspects of minimalism lies in the clearing of emotional clutter—letting go of toxic relationships and the emotional baggage that weighs us down. This process, though challenging, is essential for personal growth, well-being, and the creation of a life that aligns with our deepest values.

Emotional clutter, much like physical clutter, can accumulate over time. It often takes the form of relationships that drain our energy, unresolved conflicts, lingering resentments, and unhealed wounds from the past. These emotional burdens can lead to feelings of stress, anxiety, and overwhelm, hindering our ability to live fully and joyfully. Just as a cluttered home can make us feel suffocated and disorganised, emotional clutter can cloud our minds, making it difficult to find peace and clarity.

The first step in clearing emotional clutter is to recognise its presence in our lives. This requires an honest and introspective evaluation of our relationships and emotional landscape. We must ask ourselves difficult questions: Are there relationships that consistently leave us feeling drained, unappreciated, or hurt? Do we find ourselves holding onto past grievances, unable to forgive or move on? Are there unresolved issues that continue to occupy our thoughts and affect our emotional well-being? By acknowledging the existence of emotional clutter, we open the door to addressing it.

One of the most significant sources of emotional clutter is toxic relationships. These are relationships that are characterised by negativity, manipulation, lack of respect, or emotional harm. Toxic relationships can take many forms— they may be with friends, family members, romantic partners, or even colleagues. What they have in common is their detrimental impact on our mental and emotional health. Holding onto such relationships can create a sense of emotional clutter that prevents us from thriving and living authentically.

Evaluating our relationships with a minimalist mindset involves identifying those that are toxic or no longer serve us. This is not an easy process, as it often involves confronting uncomfortable truths and making difficult decisions. However, it is a necessary step towards emotional freedom and well-being. As we assess our relationships, we should consider how each one affects our emotional state, whether it aligns with our values, and whether it contributes positively to our lives. Relationships that consistently bring us pain, stress, or a sense of inadequacy may need to be re-evaluated.

Letting go of toxic relationships is a deeply personal and often challenging decision. It requires courage, self-compassion, and a commitment to our own well-being. However, it is important to approach this process with mindfulness and empathy, both for ourselves and for the other person involved. Ending or distancing ourselves from a toxic relationship does not necessarily mean cutting someone out of our lives abruptly or without consideration. Instead, it involves setting healthy boundaries, communicating our needs, and, when necessary, gradually creating distance.

Compassion plays a crucial role in this process. It is essential to recognise that letting go of a relationship is not about blame or judgment, but about self-care and the preservation of our emotional health. We can acknowledge the positive aspects of the relationship and the role it may have played in our lives while also recognising that it is no longer conducive to our growth and happiness. By approaching the situation with compassion, we can navigate the process with greater ease and minimise the emotional turmoil that often accompanies such decisions.

Clearing emotional clutter is not limited to toxic relationships; it also involves addressing unresolved emotional baggage. This includes past experiences that continue to haunt us, unhealed wounds, and unresolved conflicts that linger in our minds. Carrying this emotional baggage can prevent us from moving forward and fully embracing the present. The process of letting go involves acknowledging these feelings, working through them—perhaps with the help of a therapist or trusted confidant—and ultimately releasing them.

The act of clearing emotional clutter is liberating. As we let go of toxic relationships and emotional baggage, we create space in our lives for positivity, growth, and authentic connections. This process allows us to focus on relationships that are truly meaningful and nurturing—those that bring joy, support, and a sense of belonging. Surrounding ourselves with positive, supportive individuals who align with our values not only enhances our well-being but also reinforces our commitment to living intentionally and authentically.

Moreover, as we clear emotional clutter, we cultivate a greater sense of self-awareness and emotional resilience. We learn to recognise and honour our own needs, set healthy boundaries, and make decisions that reflect our commitment to our own well-being. This self-awareness empowers us to build and maintain relationships that are healthy, respectful, and mutually enriching.

The benefits of clearing emotional clutter extend beyond our personal well-being. When we are free from the weight of toxic relationships and unresolved emotions, we are better able to contribute positively to the lives of others. We can engage in our relationships with greater empathy, understanding, and presence, creating a ripple effect of positivity and connection.

In embracing the minimalist approach to emotional clutter, we are not only simplifying our emotional lives but also creating a foundation for deeper, more meaningful relationships. We are making a conscious choice to prioritise our mental and emotional health, to invest in relationships that nurture us, and to let go of those that do not. This process is an essential aspect of living with intention, authenticity, and joy.

By releasing the weight of emotional clutter, we open ourselves to the possibility of living a life that is not only more peaceful and fulfilling but also more aligned with our true selves. It is a journey of self-discovery, healing, and growth—one that leads to greater emotional freedom, resilience, and happiness.

Sharing the Path of Simplicity

Becoming a minimalist involves deep self-examination. You look at the whole of your life, make certain changes in the way of life and be of integrity with your decisions and what you value the most. To a large number of people, the principle of leading a simple life involves both decluttering of their living spaces and lifestyle change, which makes counseling and coaching particularly difficult. It is undeniable that conversions from a material manner of living to the simple way are difficult. One of the major challenges of talking about minimalism is how to confront these new values with the people around us who do not have the same view. There may be family, friends, or partners, but minimalism requires the correct level of flat if one wants to communicate openly. Truth be told, there can be interpersonal conflicts among them on the topic. Finding real satisfaction "My main motivations for pursuing a minimalist lifestyle include my zeal for encountering better clarity, purpose and peace." This is mostly because the trending fast-moving consumer culture has initiated a yearning in some people to have time to actually grow inwardly and have wonderful relationships. The fastest way to the root of the problem could be either of the suggested activities or physical life changes, or it may well be both activities and physical changes. Still, the drive will always be freeing oneself from having to keep up with the traditions. A change in mental paths will bring about reactions that range from interest to confusion or even objections to a situation that is unusual. We must stress the idea, though, that no one will rush into this change; the fact that not everyone will immediately get it or will feel comfortable about the transformation. Moreover, it is the communication that servant." You must not fall into such a trap, however. Instead, you must convey the fact that you prioritize the fulfillment of your needs. You should also clarify that these needs and goals are specific to you, and so it should be your personal choice. In such manner, you still are not imposing your position on anybody else. Rather, from opening yourself, you encourage participation and exchange of ideas instead of building a defensive shield against opposing views.

The first step to introducing minimalistic living ideas should be to be sensitive and accepting of the way the other person looks at things. Understand that other people are different. They are motivated by different things and prioritize different things, thus, their thoughts and judgments of your life are influenced by them. Instead of advocating the lifestyle of companies to replace limb-based skins you must as pheasants live in harmony with the environment. By sharing your experiences openly, you create room for conversation and research rather than dispute which often leads to defensive behaviors.

When you discuss minimalism with family, friends, or partners, it's better to emphasize the positive part of the lifestyle rather than the part you are giving up. For instance, you may describe minimalism as the principle that has enabled you to concentrate on the things that make you happy, reduce stress and amass more meaningful relationships with people. What I have just discussed is fulfilled by the main content of the sentence. By stating the benefits you have had, you can make it clear to others that minimalism is not a deprivation but a way to have a better life. Moreover, this allays the misconceptions or apprehensions that others may have about minimalism being too procedural; strict; or devoid of joy.

However, it is crucial to be ready for potential difficulties and invalidations that may emerge, as well. To some, the whole ideology of minimalism might be a challenge to their deep-seated beliefs in success, happiness, and self-identity, particularly if these beliefs are grounded in the material prosperity or social standing. The most sensitive thing in such situations would be your patience and empathy. The idea is to remember that transformation is not easy, and everyone is on a different learning curve. Besides, instead of persuading others to embrace minimalism, you can articulate your values with respect by implying that others might take a different route.

Studying limits is yet another influencing issue of keeping your simple life clear, particularly when you are clashing with social pressures or other opinions. The gatherings, family unions, or even traditions in your community are some of the mechanisms that can trigger the positions where you are under your minimalism commitment. Here are the additional ways mentioned to elaborate the main argument. For instance, there might be a case when you are put under pressure to join in the gift-exchanging process, buy unnecessary accessories, or get involved with activities that are against your principles. In such moments, the clearer and lovelier you are in expressing your limits, the simpler the other people will understand your point of view. It is not about making difference between you and the others, its about respecting your identity and still keep your relationship ongoing.

To avoid this situation, an excellent way is to present various options that are in line with your minimalism principles. Thus, instead of a physical item, you can ask for items such as experiences, moneys donated to charities, or times spent together. In this regard, you can explain that you are absolutely against the idea of piling up extra stuff in your cellar. This can be done through a "no-gift" policy or practical and consumable gifts suggestions. By providing alternatives, you will be able to partake in social customs without compromising your principles, and you may even encourage others to think about other ways of celebration and appreciation.

The technique of presenting minimalistic values through conversation can also serve as a platform for more profound relations fostered by honesty and heartfelt communication. When you express your personal goals and experiences with minimalism, you show others how you perceive life. They get to see what is most valuable to you, and they become closer to you on a deeper level than they were before. In fact, such a provocative display of vulnerability is a key that opens the door to genuine exchange of thoughts about matters that are essential to a meaningful life, especially values, goals, and life choices. At the same time, the process can also initiate a sense of solidarity, as others can parallelize your walk with minimalism, if not taking it up themselves.

Furthermore, by living in alignment with your values in a transparent and genuine way, you may become the catalyst of the self-reflection of others to see good as their primary goal. After all, minimalism is not a uniform approach, but a personal philosophy that can be changed to reflect individual necessities and positions. Small modifications or dramatic lifestyle alterations can give space to others to learn and develop creativity and flexibility which in the end can lighten their loads. In this case, someone else's dedication to minimalism may ripple out a change beyond themselves and bring a more positive impact on the people around them.

A minimalist lifestyle can be adopted without people's approval or understanding of the decision of the individual in question. The thoughts of others do not matter. What matters most is that you stay true to your own values and ideas, even when confronted by contrary opinions or when social pressures are at their peak. By adopting certain techniques, you not only demonstrate by example that intentional and fulfilling life can be lived outside of external social standards, but also that this can be done without a fight.

Self-esteem like this can build up your relationships as you become more convinced of the value of being genuine in your life.

Minimalistic living, in the process of making new friends and convincing family members that your way of life is valid—one of the keys—must also imply a new method of communication that prevents misunderstanding and promotes trust and warmth among family members. This is not disappearing into your own ideas while standing your ground, but incorporating the given opinions yet emphasizing what is common. This way, the conversation will be more constructive, and respect is agreed. Compassion, patience, and honesty are the qualities that can be used by us while talking with friends and family. These can be the key to forming stronger and more meaningful relationships with those around you, even if your views on minimalism differ.

The minimalistic journey is essentially about self-discovery and relations. During the process, as you will delve into your values further and find ways to communicate them powerfully, you will also be given a chance to be part of the shared process that enhances both your and others' lives. Through letting others know about your beliefs in a compassionate and understandable way, you are not merely showing that you are committed to simplicity, but you also are providing them with the possibility to experience a more purposeful and mindful life.

Living Simply in a Social World

The path of becoming minimalist usually starts with a genuine wish of a person to simplify life, cope with stress, and pay attention to the most important aspects of life. Still, as one gets deeper and the lifestyle takes more space, the challenge of keeping interconnectedness with others and being a minimalist becomes more visible. In social events—the case when we are parties, meetings, gatherings, or celebrations we understand that they are settings with expectations that contradict the minimalist consciousness. The trick here is to find a middle way which will enable you could bigger these along without burdening your value of simplicity and purposefulness.

Minimalism is a mindful process when dealing with people in social settings. In some cases, social interactions can be tied up with certain cultural traditions and customs that might not be in accordance with the philosophy of minimalism. As an example, attending a party might result in the unnecessary storage of items that are given as gifts. Similarly, hanging out with friends may be a barrier to becoming a minimalist who is anti-consumption and the resulting waste. Nonetheless, one cannot overlook the fact that minimalism is not about being anti-social or renouncing leisure activities' part. Instead, one can engage in the activities and get happiness when living according to their principles.

Whereas giving companies at parties the above-mentioned have constraints as well, the gift economy has a particular effect on sustainability according to the Community Research and Action. The latter often feels like conforming to the culture of excess and acquiring material possessions. They might fear losing the respect of their peers, finding a partner, or even the simple fact that they themselves might regret their decisions later. To begin with, fear and anxiety connected to the engagement of such social situations have to be embraced as part of the sociocultural context in which these conflicts must be resolved. The first step in battling this issue is realizing that these pressures are just figments of your imagination and one can navigate the social life without prejudice and judgment.

One of the ways where you can find a balance between minimalism and being connected to social activities is to pick the events and gatherings you would like to attend. You don't have to accept every invitation and you are not supposed to participate in each social event. By assessing which of these events are truly significant to you and which of these events are in accordance with your values, you can decide more consciously how you will spend your time and energy. Practicing a selective way of meeting people through co-operation therefore you get to express your connection with society through available social infrastructure while also keeping your balance in life. The most common topic about life is related to the act of giving. Usually, minimalists are in that dilemma of how to agree with the culture without promoting material prosperity. One of the solutions is talking about your values and offering the alternatives to the regular gifts. For example, propose the idea of giving experiences rather than items—like concert tickets, a gift card for an outing, or a donation to a charitable organization. These gifts are minimalist in nature and also the recipients will always remember them and their lives will be enriched more than keeping some items.

Friendship over materiality can be promoted through suspended or no exchanging of gifts. This method, also known as gift negotiation, can symbolize the giving of a gift that is not the same as the physical giving of it. One way that tentative minimalists (minimalists who are on the fence about the lifestyle) passionately adjoin themselves to other individuals who are avid environmentalists is by commemorating giraffes. The removal of items is related to reinventing the idea of giving, instead of buying. Thus, older items, even with very few desirable traits, can sometimes be incredibly useful for fixing or redesigning new units: rather than exposing new resources to the depletion of the earth, consumers can thus opt for repairing and redesigning.

On the whole, this comedy leads to an amazing turn of events when he loses his toys but gains his dad. The overall theme of the story is the importance of friendship to real happiness. When he is forced to leave his belongings, he realizes that he can still play and have fun. In a negative way, the accident caused him to need medical treatment and caused damage to his car. He was taken to the hospital and, despite the serious injuries, the driver of the other car was arrested.

You can dine out, that is another social activity, which is relatively hard for minimalists, especially due to the issues related to the cost and overconsumption, that you might fine. Nevertheless, along with your friends and relatives, it is a very lovely opportunity to bond, but you should not forget how to be aware of your spending, e.g. how frequent are the eateries you visit and their environmental friendliness. Building up social ties and maintaining minimalism could be through the following the idea of doing less but with more mindfully approach, and a way to do this is to select only such restaurants as are engaged in, for instance, an environment-friendly lifestyle, local sourcing of ingredients, or the fair treatment of employees. Additionally, you can propose the ideas of hosting or attending potlucks, where everyone chips in a dish that makes a more communal and less costly dining experience.

Involvement in the luxury items and goods-seeking activities that characterize capitalist life, such as exclusive parties or luxe shopping feasts, can also become a matter of discomfort among minimal people. Here, it would be more convenient for you to shift your focus to the stuff that is not superfluous, such as the ability to connect and bond with people as well as to be part of a great cause. If, however, the copious consumption aspect of the event or the contradicting attitude of some aspects of the event is still creeping in your mind, then you need to set restrictions for yourself—e.g. you might decide to limit your participation to the chosen activities or politely explain your excuse to those parts that you don't gel with. This way, you can still be with people and will not be compelled to abandon your minimalist lifestyle even though some of the displayed behavior might disturb you.

The ultimate goal of life is to live simply and thoughtfully, not complicating it through unnecessary commitments. What I am getting at is whenever we agree to a social event that will lead us to stress, fatigue, and take away our peace and tranquility, it is total against what minimalism stands for. It is, therefore, necessary to review the social events that fill your weekly schedule and then to prioritize ones that give you pleasure to be a part of them, satisfaction, and means of direct interpersonal communication. By this, you will necessarily be saying no to open invitations that are more about your presence than your participation in the activity. This, in turn, will allow you to partition your life in a way that only the bought-into activities and relationships become your main occupations.

Minimalism, at its base, has to do with purposeful and intended life. Such philosophy is applicable to the social part of lives in the same way as to the rest of living. It's about the kind of decisions that demonstrate your values and result in a life that is more uncomplicated, clear, and full of sense. Instead of withdrawing from social life, minimalism urges us to communicate with others authentically and responsibly and thus be able to fulfill ourselves and have higher standards of life, away from consumerism and social demands.

Furthermore, through your daily practices, by being transparent about your minimalist values and being sincere, you not only can live your minimalistic lifestyle, but also you have the power to direct your environment. Your line of social behavior—such as your choices of travel, your decision to eat out, etc.—can be the vehicle that inspires others to look back and review their conduct and choices. This domino effect will in turn extend to your social groups, promoting healthy and intentional interactions that facilitate the establishment of a community that has compassion and depth as its key values and is not obsessed with owning more things.

By doing minimalism in the social world, you are not only following your values but also enjoy the more meaningful cultivation of relationships and experiences. It is in the middle of the one dosage of social living and the dedication to ease that the complication lies. Handling social situations mindfully, intentionally, and with open communication can be a way to turn socializing into a learning and personal development tool.

Being the guy who chooses minimalism and has a social life is, in the end, the same as being the person who reflects himself and values the most. It refers to the world as a place where life becomes less materialistic, and more humorous, in the way that you can feel free enough to be who you want and be with them. It's more connecting to always pragmatic and feature the aspects of humanity in connection with relationships and experiences that fill you with happiness. By this way you can achieve a lively social environment that perfectly corresponds to your minimalistic motivation, one that not only nourishes you but also your simple and intentional way of livng at the same time.

The Depths of Simple Intimacy

In a world where more often than not, the ties of lives of humans are in turmoil due to the pressures associated with progress the minimalists' principles of living, still, detailed inhabitants on the trust of relationships whether or not it be a lover, a brother or a new friend, ideas that suggest minimalism do provide a pathway. At the heart of minimalism lies the idea of removing the irrelevant and concentrating on the essentials. When used in relation to human relationships, this can be a life-changing means of communication with our loved ones through the creation of an authentic space, replete with truthfulness, honesty, and intentionality, as the basis of true friendship.

Minimalism is a life lesson on how to live with precision of thought and action, making it clear that love and relationship dynamics cannot be done without developing wisdom. Especially within marriage or in a close relationship, the emphasis is on being thoughtful and kind to people in walking and talking, as well as nurturing individuals' creativity and happiness. Through accepting and applying minimalism, the situation is created where both spouses alike feel listened to, known fully, and strongly relate on the internal level.

The total transparency and trust in the relationship triangle when it comes to the usage of honesty and mere fairness is what makes minimalism authentic and a proper therapy for couples. In a minimalist relationship, honesty is directly related to vulnerability and open communication. It involves passive disposal of personal and private thoughts, emotions, and necessities without bothering for evaluation of self-judgment or the rarest rejection. This level of openness builds trust, as it provides relationship partners the chance to see the others' inner worlds and offer meaningful support. When both individuals are determined to be frank and forgiving, a behavior pattern is set up in which the emotional bond is lightened and flourish.

One more essential factor alongside accountability is the ability to clearly represent one's plans and desires within the union. Taking on excessive possessions leads to no goals, but only forces our hands to think about what is important and what is not. Integrity in the course of a relationship can be shown by being involved, being vocal, asking questions, and giving feedback. If both partners are honest and discuss what they want, trust and mutual support between them are established which help in building a healthy relationship. Mutual clarity, along with mutual trust, will make a couple feel united as one and help them confidently deal with any issues.

Yet another aspect of relationships becoming minimalist is the removal of distractions that block real connections. Nowadays, the technology, social media, and materialism get in the way of human connection, in which the latter has already been threatened. Minimalism is inviting you to streamline your lifestyle, to chuck out the distracting elements that stand in the way of enjoyable relationships. We can get more immersed in people-to-people encounters by dialing back our screen time, less material focus, and meeting based instead on real life emotional lows and highs. We then grow and get to experience more of the deepest type of connection and closeness to one another.

Clearing the way for fewer distractions endorses more in-depth, actual contact. The mere fact that our minds are not wandering all over or that we are not attached to our tiny gadgets all the time, automatically puts us in a position of giving young people the gift of the fullness of our attention. This is the main way on how a couple can relax, nurture intimacy, and demonstrate the value of the time spent together. Whether we bond through collective activities or sincere talks, or just silently relish each other's presence, the moments of presence are the ones that tie us together for eternity and sustain the best of memories.

However, this particular topic is more connected with the feeling that folks receives when they are not afraid to disclose their true gender identity. The main things that are discussed in a relationship are the central issues—namely, being real, the bond, and the meaning of such an experience to both partners. It thus means that the two of them are free to be themselves, to disclose their thoughts and emotions openly, without being afraid of the most terrible consequences, such as criticism or disapproval. If we are able to be comfortable and happy as we are, the chances of our innermost thoughts and aspirations being shared with our loved ones and the consequent establishment of a deep emotional connection are greatly increased.

For a long-lasting bond, emotional intimacy is a fundamental requirement. Emotional intimacy is the sense of nearness and understanding the couple experiences due to sharing their real selves, knowing that they will be loved and acknowledged for what they are. Minimalism serves to develop this intimacy by doing away with all the obstacles that are of causing pain, which typically includes the need to make a good impression, fear of vulnerability, and the lure of materialism. By doing away with these barriers, we create a space that allows for the love, trust, and connection to flourish.

Scheduling time for each other is a further important ingredient of caring love and loyalty. In a fast-paced world like the one we live in, it is easy to inadvertently overlook the significance of spending time with our loved ones, as we are often preoccupied with work, duties, and other responsibilities. Yet, minimalism consistently emphasizes the need to concentrate on what really matters and modern stress and strain can be eliminated from the surface of lives of people. Thus, most of the time, relationships receive the most attention. Through taking deliberate action to attend to our significant others and family, we demonstrate to them that they are our top priority. Young couples can arrange lovey-dovey evenings at home for the purpose of closer connection, shared family dinners, and just getting together at home for quality time during which they can learn the art of loving each other.

In point of fact, participating in group activities also helps to close the bond between companions and family members. Shared activities, regardless of whether they are hobbies, adventure or alternatively, daily routines, are the heartbeat of bonding. Shared activities are also relics of memory that are grounded in love and unity within the relationship. It is perfectly simple to perceive that they are not fancy and expensive activities; in fact, they are the times when people have the most fun and enjoy life fully. You could take a stroll, stir together a meal, or work on a creative project—these are joint actions that fortify the emotional connection and yield timeless experiences.

Another aspect of minimalism that allows families or couples to discover their common purpose is to honour the values they both are concerned with that also guide them. Both partners devoted to living simply and intentionally can shape a lifestyle that mirrors their shared values. That could mean discussing problems about expenditure of the main breadwinner, amount of time children should spend, and who gets more/ gets more time with. Through harmonizing values and goals, the pair will be able to interact positively and grow in togetherness, thereby creating an inclusive and harmonious life where both lovers are cared for and satisfied.

In a less complex bond, the important aspect is mutual respect and understanding. If each of them is directed towards areas of real interest, they should naturally respect each other's needs, opinions, and peculiarities while also being graceful about the different sides. This respect is the base of a loving, prosperous relationship, where both persons are not only accepted but also feel important and valuable. The ability of either of the partners to fully know and appreciate each other's views, challenges, and dreams is also a key aspect of a stronger bond and a more supportive complicity.

Indeed, minimalism goes further than being a common decorative trend; the philosophy has paved a new path to understand the industrial culture and the consumerism that it creates. It suggests that what seems to be the abundance we can't get enough of, is nothing but an illusion. It is the reason why people are so anxious even when living, for the most part, in comfort. The very stuff that is supposed to make us happy is often the reason for our anxiety. Therefore, the fewer things we have, the less we are bothered by what we have and want yet as they are too costly we can't afford or they just make some false kind of happiness. In order to live in a society of things, you have always to say you're going to purchase next, prioritize and be sensitive to the visual image representation of your new purchase when the old things are hidden in the elderly houses.

Chapter 7

Minimalism in Different Cultures

The minimalism phenomenon as a lifestyle and a philosophy is now the hot potato worldwide as it has its own fair share of publicity in recent decades. However, thus the simplicity of minimalism may seem to be very clear—by favoring simplicity and not allowing abundance—the way it is realized and practiced can be very different from one culture to another. In this entry, the many faces of minimalism in different parts of the globe are shown and the different cultural contexts that give shape and color to this approach to living are also laid out

In connection with modern Western civilization, minimalism is usually associated with consumerism and materialistic values that have become dominant in the most advanced regions of the world. In a lot of places in the West, minimalism is viewed as a cure for the mess of life as we live it—thus, living a life of minimalism becomes a way to control everything and have a calm and peaceful environment. But the roots of minimalism are way longer than this recent brand suggests and its representation is not one-dimensional. Thus, the principles of minimalism are not unique to one time or place but have been used in many such cultures that have used it as a concept of addressing the same human concern for material wealth being the basis for happiness for long periods long before the word "minimalism" became a hit with the young generation.

The main difference in the perception of minimalism can be found in the approach of Eastern and Western beings. One of the significant ways in which the approach to simplicity via minimalism is distinct is the difference between the Eastern and Western interpretations. In many Asian countries, minimalism is interwoven with the spiritual and philosophical sides of life. Renouncing the excesses of life is already considered as a path to enlightenment or self-discovery, drawing from traditions and philosophies that include, among others, Zen Buddhism, Taoism, Hinduism. In these societies, minimalism is not just about getting rid of physical stuff but it also includes learning the detachment technique, being on hold in full consciousness, and living perfectly with the environment. This, of course, is in contrast with the Western strategy, which is the most popular one (in terms of practical benefits of minimalism) such as the art of decluttering, stress reduction, and the increase of working efficiency.

The impact of Eastern philosophy on the philosophy of minimalism is best demonstrated by the popularity of Zen Buddhism, which is, after all, about the importance of simplicity, mindfulness, and the absence of diversions. Practicing biofeedback-like meditation, a technique that rids oneself of thought processes, is a reflection of what Gary Weber refers to as "dyamani"'s ski trip. The Zen monochrome approach, made up of simple shapes, open spaces, and no decorations, has also been a decision-making factor in Western design and lifestyle trends along with the minimalist architecture and "less is more" style in interior design.

Otherwise, Western minimalism frequently comes as an antidote to the demands of consumer culture. The previous two centuries have witnessed an unexampled increase in consumerism rooted in mass production, advertising, and the abundance of goods. That way has given us a society that is characterized through overconsumption the choice of material goods is often seen as the measure of a person's success and happiness. Nevertheless, as people have been increasingly enlightened to the adverse environmental effects, financial worries and a sense of emptiness caused by the relentless pursuit of consumerism, many have turned to minimalism as a life raft amidst the prevailing materialistic culture. Gradually, this community has come to regard minimalism as the answer to their lives through the streamlining of their lives, removing the clutter, and holding on to what life is really all about, maybe health, maybe relationships or maybe personal growth.

Although minimalistic fundamentals such as radicality, specificity, and consciousness are identified principles, they are actualized in quite different places by different social settings. Minimalism in cities offers at one and the same time a variety of challenges and benefits. Thus, the poor urban living conditions have lessened the minimalism lifestyle that the urban population leads in lessening the spaciousness and air quality of the cities, as an upsurge in the city dwelling practice has effected over municipalities in the last decade. The urban minimalism trend has gathered pace, especially among young professionals looking to make the most of the silence and the order that they have set up in the middle of city life. So the small-space living, the co-living arrangements, and the rising of the interest in digital minimalism, which is the thought-provoking approach for the people who only utilize technology and social media when crucial and compare it with other more satisfying, less virtual activities, are the signs of such a growing tendency.

Minimalism is demonstrated in a different way in rural and old traditions. In many rural areas, simplicity is not a lifestyle choice but a necessity. For example, agricultural communities have been practicing minimalism through self-sufficiency, resourcefulness and a close connection to the land for a very long time. The traditional rituals often express minimalist values such as to keep within one's possibilities, to minimize waste and to realize what is truly important. The context, in this case, is that minimalism is not about the abandonment of the modern conveniences that society offers, but the way of life that is sustainable and culturally rich.

Moreover, minimalism is spreading globally and such globalization has prompted curiosity about the ways in which this lifestyle is being adopted and adapted in various parts of the world. From the Scandinavian idea of "lagom," which proposes a middle path and harmony, through the Japanese tradition of "wabi-sabi," which exploits the aesthetic of the imperfect, the transient, the abandoned, to minimalism, which appears in different cultures --all of these demonstrate that minimalism can be expressed in numerous cultures. The world-wide nature of these movements points to the diverse applicability of minimalism as well as the fact that individuals from different cultural backgrounds can bridge new interpretations and practices to minimalism.

Nonetheless, it is worth mentioning that globalization of the minimalist movement is fraught with various questions about cultural appropriation, inclusivity, and the looming possibility of the movement being turned into something commercial that taints its integrity. The popularization of minimalism might possibly engulf the underpinning of its deep philosophical roots in superficiality or commercial interest. For instance, the focus on the minimalism of aesthetics in Western fashion and design might result in a mere dress of minimalism that seeks to give it an attractive look as opposed to a substantive one. Also, the trend of minimalist products in the market like the new, high-fashion furniture or "eco-friendly" products is an irony to the main idea of minimalism which is about withdrawal and content gaining.

Minimalism, social structures, and cultural norms are intersecting on an important level, and this combination is the most significant to analyze. In some cultures, minimalism is a way to dismantle the traditional norms of family, community, and social status. For example, in societies where the place one occupies in the social hierarchy is defined by material status, the choice to live a simple life might be considered a very far away option or a sabotage of the system. But you can't possibly be a person who has the claim of simplicity and not demonstrate the concerned values. This is due to the fact that success is no longer seen in the material sphere alone but in capacities for self-management and family well-being. In contrast, people who choose to live this way are often able to make a statement that goes against the material sufficiency-based normatives. Besides, minimalism serves as a way of attracting the positive social values one needs to exercise. As playing the roles at a grand company party a person can be just as effective in the minimalist clothes of less of everything such as an item of new, Shawna's apple, and designer cut-offs. Such a situation is also favorable for putting on a videoconference where everyone is silent as everyone is trying to make the best words to break the silence.

Also, the roles of religion and spirituality are very important in the development and implementation of minimalist practices across world cultures. Many of the world's religious traditions such as Christianity, Islam, and Hinduism are a source of simplicity, modesty, and even detachment from material possession with others considered it as a means of spiritual self-improvement. The teachings that these religions deliver intersect with minimalism, implying that the need for a simple life is not a fashion that relates to modern times only it is a universal wish that human beings have since ancient times. In this regard, spirituality and minimalism are closely connected; therefore, all we need to do is to focus on one and explore the practices attached to that to have a complete understanding of respective fields.

The exploration of the interplay between different cultural frameworks and minimalism reveals that simplicity offers a lot of different solutions because one shoe doesn't fit everybody. In contrast, minimalism can be a flexible and adjustable concept that can be customized according to the wants and the situations of the people and the communities around the world. Actually, there is a city where one can feel relaxed and indoor as urbanization has killed the fresh air leisure places, a village where nature is the main attraction but also there is a spiritual place. Minimalism is such an amazing opportunity to reorient human beings to simple, mindful, and happy living.

In this chapter, we will investigate how different cultures explain and practice simplicity, and we will see how diverse cultures perceive and execute minimalism. Starting from Zen-minimalism that is found in Japan to the eco-conscious minimalism of the Scandinavians, we shall bring out the tapestry of minimalism in different cultures found around the globe. We will also reflect on the issues and prospects that arise when minimalism is used in different cultural contexts, and how this movement can be more inclusive, sustainable, and respectful of its diverse roots.

Through the (cultural) angle, we can strengthen our love for the lifestyle and find it to be a very constructive element in creating both personal and global change. If you are just getting started or you have already been practicing minimalism for a long time, this various cultures' approach to minimalism will provide you with new thoughts and ideas how to experience life with less and be more purposeful.

The Cultural Dimensions of Minimalism

Minimalism, as an idea and a practice, has turned into a global phenomenon, but the manner in which it is received and used varies a lot among the different cultures. On the one hand, the West usually goes minimalism through a cleaner and consumerism-reducing route, while on the other hand, the East has been living the principles of minimalism for a long time in their daily life, as well as in spiritual and philosophical questioning. These dissimilarities of understanding and practice provide unique perspectives on how different cultural constructs influence our minimalist approaches and also underscore the potential for mutual cross-cultural learning and enrichment.

Minimalism is one of the core beliefs in the eastern part of the world, and it is mainly manifested through the spirituality and the philosophy they developed over the years. The most popular Zen Buddhist idea seems to be the simplest one, with a focus on simple life, an act of care, and the idea that the main obstacles to inner peace and enlightenment are all our unnecessary distractions. Minimalism to the Zen masters is not just about the giving away of the material stuff, which is thought to be the physical indicator of mental splinters; the donation of mental peace is also included in the process. This clarification of the mind is the precondition to be able to go through the spiritual build-up and get to root the ideas being offered.

The visual art of the Zen style is also very impressive. Zen gardens as well as the The Essence of Joy

Less is more, and minimalism is the quantum leap in the process to attain joy. Minimalism in itself is a concept that encourages human beings to look beyond the external success that is superficial and begin the journey on a more intrinsic level of happiness. The journey these people embark on the road toward simplifying their lives brings with it the awareness that there is a complex relationship between material things and their lives. They are themselves happy being with the others and then using the rest of the space for their activities, rather than having everything crowded and suffocated.

Minimalist happiness is not a masochistic act of deprivation but a deliberate choice to live in such a way that it creates the least distress possible, even if it is the hardest thing to do. It teaches individuals to critically analyze the pursuit of success-through the accumulations of goods according to societal norms-and the associated activities that promulgate such socialization. A shift of thinking from material possessions to the profound meaning of life can promote a new age of well-being in personal lives that also spread into other parts of the society.

One of the most impactful aspects of minimalism is the liberty to break free from the bonds imposed by society to keep up with its expectations externally. We are free from excessive belongings and commitments when we let go of those we do not really need, and develop space for self-actualization and self-discovery. Through the process of recovery from gadget addiction, the truth becomes apparent. The joy arising from the better communication, the peace of the mind due to the clean house, or the happiness of pursuing, for example, a project far exceeds pleasure of just taking a time good.

At the same time, leading a lifetime of minimalism happiness, which is a little different from traditional methods of assessing happiness, is rather a complex endeavor. The conventional standards of living- success in economics, the magnificence of the properties can hardly catch the essence of such a lifestyle. Therefore, we should find ways that show the quality of our internal environment. A manufacturer can provide tools such as self-assessment sheets to be used as a means to the same end of grading work and keeping track of personal development. These may include, for one, releasing periodical literature in which a group member expresses a moment of contentment, a sense of purpose, and overall life satisfaction.

Additionally, observing a reduction in stress can be employed as [an] alternative effective technique to measure the benefits of minimalism. It is commonly found that the process of decluttering living standards significantly aids people to cope better with anxiety and other mental health concerns. It is pertinent to consider a number of procedures such as charting sleep quality, monitoring cortisol levels, or noting incidences of symptoms like: headaches, irritability, and anxiety if one wants to be absolutely sure of the conversion. The fresh mental clarity that accompanies the minimalist way of life can lead to better judgment and more power in controlling one's life.

Mental recovery becomes the most significant resource that minimalism grant. One interesting initial finding that has been produced is that the path of the people living this life is not only maintained but they also develop a new sense of awareness. The way a person spends the freed-up time and whether they have more time now to do the important things in life can be indicators of the positive effects of the lifestyle. Are you now more open to hobbies you had put aside for a long time? Are you now spending more quality time with loved ones? These reallocations can directly influence one's sense of well-being.

'Eudaimonia' is one of the concepts which are often understood as human flourishing or prosperity, its application can provide helpful insight into how minimalism can influence the type of happiness felt- it differs significantly from simple pleasure. Happiness based on pleasure and the avoidance of pain is considered hedonic happiness whereas eudaimonic wellbeing is the real feeling of contentment which arises from living a virtuous life and fulfilling one's potential. The concept of minimalism is almost identical to this in that it draws people's attention to their self-growth, their relationship to others, and the contribution to problems bigger than themselves.

Those who have embraced minimalism as a way of living get to experience and see the world from a different perspective. The constant pursuit of consumerism has been increasingly replaced by understanding the already present and a lack of too much of anything. This appreciation is one of the strongest sources of happiness, as it is independent of external situations or acquisitions. The first skill that can sustain such a person through the many facets of life is the art of having joy despite something difficult.

One must realize that the journey to minimalism and the accompanying happiness may well be the most unique for each person. What fills one with joy and happiness is different for each of us. Therefore, any attempt to come up with a scale to measure happiness here should be far from generalized. People must frequently ponder their lives, with a view to a possibility of continual appraisal and reformulation of these plans in order for them to fit the standards of lived truth and mastery.

The minimalistic effect does not spare other people relations, those at work, and the community in general. When people opt for and are more conscious of their choices and more present in relationships, they are likely to get better at interpersonal relations. The impact of the ripple effect in terms of the connection of the broader community and its consequent relationship satisfaction needs to be mentioned as well.

Success at minimalism, primarily, is the capacity to function on a comfortable level with no overwhelming factors but the items and ideas which closely comply with the individual's values and motives. It is a construction of a life where the outer world reflects the inner values of the person where they are free to do whatever they want and enjoy themselves without the burden of the rest of this world. This parallels the human psyche by creating an experience that is both joyful and profoundly enduring.

As life goes on, difficulties continue, and life continues to be tricky with the nonstop message- the more, the better, minimalism has brought about a breath of fresh air. It is a stark reminder that happiness and fulfillment are not in the heap of goodies but in the beauty of life, the growth of relationships, and the congruence of our actions with our highest principles. The rule of psychological happiness and the absence of pain that is activated by factors in a person is not the case with the sense of well-being; it is based on the right-to-existence ethical value system and the fulfillment of the highest potential.apanese tea ceremonies, and Zen Buddhist architecture are dominantly centered around the principle of simplicity as well as the effective use of the empty space as a strong idea. Here, minimalism is not just the absence of something but the presence of something—main and emphasized element which brings unity and peace. The act of mindfulness, which foster people in a non-judgmental, open, and mindful way to the present moment, goes hand in hand and by so doing it stimulates and promotes present action in the way it enhances focus and intentionality.

On the other hand, the Western minimalist movement often dawns as a response to the overpowered modern consumer culture. The 20th and 21st centuries have been a stage of the most unbelievable rise in the production and consumption of goods, which means a real selling point that consists of getting more and more possessions is often advocated for the feeling of joy and pleasure. This customer-centric thinking has brought about the excessive mess, which has in turn worsened the pollution and the loss of meaningful human interactions. For this reason, Western minimalism usually takes the practical route of reducing the waste and energy and cleaning up life as a means to counteract the negative effects of consumerism.

Western minimalism, nonetheless, is strongly tied up with the phrase "less is more," that was made famous by architect Ludwig Mies van der Rohe. This concept proposes selectively eliminating the superfluous in a field such as architecture, design, which also applies to getting rid of excessive possessions so that the needed and necessary order and clarification are achieved. The emphasis is on the advantages of minimized consumption—like time savings, less money, being more decision-maker—sufficient to spill impetus for minimalist ideas and approaches. This path often involves aesthetics, in which you go for a minimalist design with clean lines, neutral shades, and free circulation of atmosphere for calmness and easiness.

At the same time, such differences exist, some significant parallels are found in the minimalism theories of the East and the West. They are both aware of the power of simplicity and of the convenience that it entails to leave aside separatrix and dive deep into the core of one's commitment. however, they often vary in terms of reasoning and basis, which is commensurate with the cultural baggage of these scenes.

Eastern minimalism, from spirituality, tends to see simplicity as a route to clearing your mind so that you can see the divine or inner peace. It's a normal approach whose dimensions are physically quiet but also mentally, emotionally, and spiritually peaceful. The goal is not to just have stuff but to live with the baggage of the things that you have refused to sell or discard. Minimalism, which is a spiritual idea, you can find noticeably in practices such as meditation, mindfulness, and the pursuit of harmony with nature.

On the other hand, Western minimalism is usually more concerned with practical and material aspects of life. The idea here is to get rid of the physical mess, clear the space in which one lives, and live consciously in order to be more efficient and less stressed. Although there is a mention to the mental and emotional good sides of minimalism, these are usually said to be rankings of the practical benefits of having fewer things. Western Minimalism is often spurred by an urge to escape the stress and toxins of consumer culture, lower their environmental footprints, and self-sufficiently take charge of their own lives.

Traditional beliefs significantly influence the two differing schemes of minimalism. The Eastern region swears directly in the Eastern tradition of inner peace, mindfulness, and detachment from the material world, therefore the practice of minimalism is in that framework automatically. The act of minimalism is a spiritual discipline that is not only a lifestyle but also deeply rooted in the religious and cultural background.

The minimalism movement has become an anti-materialism reaction to the exceedingly competitive and consumption-based nature of Western cultures which have valued material success, individualism, and consumption as the main life values. The Western minimalist movement often challenges the norms of consumer society by advocating for a more intentional and sustainable way of living. This approach is both a critique of the excesses of modern life and a call to return to a simpler, more meaningful existence.

There is, however, a great deal of overlap and mutual learning within Eastern and Western takes on minimalism. A case in point is that Western minimalists pursuing spirituality and philosophy could interact with their Eastern counterparts for best practices. Through the help of this practice, Western minimalists can train and make themselves grow a lifestyle that is less complex and with a deeper feeling of peace and happiness. They can do this through the application of practices such as mindfulness, meditation, and residing in the moment rather than worrying about the past or future.

Despite the fact that Western approaches can further be added to the Eastern minimalism, the article has dealt with previously, the truth is that minimalism is not only of spiritual zeal but also in practice, it has to do with the use of lesser resources, particularly those that are toxic to our environment. The emphasis on decluttering, reducing waste, and living sustainably can complement the spiritual practices of Eastern minimalism, offering tangible tools for simplifying life in a modern context. By adding these elements to Eastern minimalism, even more people will be able to adopt it and will find it truly transformative.

The study of the comparison between the approaches of the East and West of minimalism has unveiled the fact that although the routes might differ, a common notion of a more off-course, more mindful and more connected to the things that truly matter is often the output. The main reasons why people turn towards minimalism are the following three that are spiritual growth, practical concerns, and the desire to evade the pressures of modern life. This new way of living, the minimalist approach, allows us to cut out the unnecessary elements and instead we get peace, clarity, and fulfillment through a more simple life.

Minimalism, in particular the intercultural aspects of it that are being examined, showcases the fact that there is no single "correct" way of practicing minimalism. Instead, it exists as a philosophy that can be changed and adjusted to suit the specific needs, preferences and identity of people or societies around the world. We can strengthen our practice and find novel ways to live more intentionally, mindfully and meaningfully by understanding and valuing the diverse expressions of minimalism across cultures.

The exchange of ideas between the Eastern approach and the Western approach to minimalism presents a wonderful opportunity for cross-cultural learning and collaboration. Through the development of each respective tradition's strengths we can be more holistic and open-minded towards minimalism- from a spiritual as well as a practical side. In so doing we not only enrich our lives but also contribute to a global movement that aims to achieve a more balanced, sustainable, and harmonious world.

The Sacred Path of Simplicity

Minimalism, as a rule of simplicity and an increasing movement, has its source in the spiritual and religious traditions of many cultures around the world. Even long before "minimalism" became a buzz word, various religious and spiritual practices had seen that the way of simplicity, a modest attitude, and detachment from material belongings is the only way to spiritual growth and inner peace. Of these practices, the ones in Hinduism, Christianity, Islam and indigenous beliefs are the most noteworthy and show how minimalism is not just about throwing away physical mess but rather, it is a profound spiritual way.

Asceticism is a main theme in most religious traditions that suggest the minimalist way of life. Sometimes the ascetic way, the self-denying and the escaping the pleasures of the world, will purify the soul and lead to the right spiritual master. In Hinduism, ascetic sadhus voluntarily renounce any material asset and live a life of extreme poverty, executing religious behavior such as yoga, and praying. This is called renunciation, and it is a process of overcoming the ego and achieving spiritual liberation or moksha as oppose to being a sacrifice to the ego.

Likewise, in Christianity, monasticism has constantly raised the virtues of poverty and selflessness of material wealth. Monks and nuns take vows of poverty, chastity, and obedience, living in communal settings where material possessions are shared or kept to a minimum. Such kind of lifestyle is to detach people from the material world and the things that might distract them from their connection with God. The continuous action of fasting, a common type of asceticism in Christianity, is one way some people practice spiritual minimalism in which they willfully stop eating food or others in order to purify the body, mind and also increase the spiritual connection with God.

Zuhd, or the practice of asceticism, in Islam also has a deep spiritual side to it. For a person to be truly zuhd, he must have an aversion to all material things and look at life from the other side of this world. They are asked to lead a simple life and avoid worldly amusements that are of no real value. This teaching is also evident in the actions of the Prophet who promoted a modest life and happiness, recalling that genuine wealth does not consist of material wealth but happiness of the soul. The practice of Ramadan is, namely, fasting for an entire month from the first light of the day till after the sun hours, an instrumentality by which this teaching is accomplished as it eliminates greed and ingratitude creating a hunger for spirituality and a realization that the spiritual is superior to material communed.

Indigenous spiritual beliefs of most tribes form a set of ideas with the same minimalist themes around the world. Indigenous people in most tribal communities have a common belief that nature is sacred and it is important to only take the things that one needs and to give back as much as they take. Environmental protection, known as Earth Ethic, a working hypothesis of this author, is a really close relation to both minimalism and confidence to the world, which also involves the indigenous cultures. Among the indigenous people, the allocation of resources is done through simple and efficient means and the environment is integrated with their way of life. According to the indigenous spirituality, indigenous rituals are not only about cutting down on consuming but also about a deep spiritual recognition of the interrelation of all life forms and the duty to care for the earth.

Pilgrimage is a very compelling instance of spiritual minimalism that is to be found in many religious systems. Pilgrimage entails the act of forsaking regular comforts in the quest for a holy space, which is often done by foot. It is an act of both physical and spiritual simplification, where the pilgrims rid themselves of the superfluous and concentrate on the spiritual goals of purification, penance, and connection with God. Whether it is the Hajj pilgrimage to Mecca in Islam, the Camino de Santiago in Christianity, or the Char Dham Yatra in Hinduism, these are all spiritual treks that involve the pilgrim giving up material needs so that they can focus solely on the spiritual aspect.

Fasting, a spiritual practice commonly found in many religions, is another way by which spiritual minimalism is demonstrated and it is an interconnection of simplicity and faith. Fasting is more than just avoiding food, it's a form of self-discipline and mindfulness that helps believers to put aside body needs and to concentrate on their spiritual growth. Apart from physical fasting, some religious traditions have mental fasting as well, individuals renounce their negative thoughts, words or behaviors during spiritual purification. This mental simplicity, complementing the other forms, gives an overall picture of the way minimalism is promoted within spiritual practices.

The teachings of religion also frequently stress the benefits of modesty and humility, which are in line with minimalistic principles. Modesty is a common theme in most religions, and it is not just about routine or clothing but cultivating a mind of simplicity and contentment. For Bali, the theory of "right livelihood" motivates people to live ethically and in a simple way, to avoid the occupation or lifestyle that creates only harm and excess. Tzniut, a principle in Judaism that modesty is sometimes translated as is another example of modesty as an attitude to both appearance and life. It represents a modest life that is concentrated on spiritual rather than material pursuits.

The connection of minimalism with religious and spiritual practices gives us an insight that simplicity is not just a lifestyle but a deep route to inner peace & heaven. In various religions, minimalist principles such as reducing the superfluous, concentration on the fundamental, and living life consciously engrave in the spiritual teachings, which allow the believers to live a life of clarity, purpose, and connection to the divine.

First of all, these religious and spiritual forms of minimalism offer a real firsthand learning experience to those who practice minimalism as a secular lifestyle. The emphasis on mindfulness, detachment, and intentionality in religious minimalism can prompt a deeper and more profound approach to simplicity, one that transcends the outer layers of decluttering and encompasses the spiritual aspects of life. On the other hand, through minimalism's spiritual teaching one can learn to bring to light what is the essence of simplicity, as in, not only material possessions but each dimension of one's life.

It is apparent that the current popularity of minimalism in modern society which may be interpreted as a return to similar ancient spiritual principles. As people look for ways to better themselves and look for solace and serenity, they are also rediscovering the value of the simplicity that ancient religious and spiritual teaching has long been promoting. Weather whether by meditation, fasting, or mindful living, or through an ethical lifestyle and environmental stewardships, the fundamentals of minimalism still offer the right way to experience a more fulfilled and spiritually enriched life.

The minimalism-spirituality relation provides evidence of the ubiquity of the search for simplicity and, consequently, the mutual language of simplicity. All around the world in every religion, there is a shared perception that true peace of mind and fulfillment are not derived from the accumulation of material abundance but rather the inner qualities one obtains thus it is as a result of self-cultivation. This parallel existence is transcultural thus people can widely enjoy the transformative power of living easily with no barriers of faith and background.

Reflecting upon the theme of minimalism in spiritual and religious concepts, simplicity turns out to be much more than a mere reduction of materialism: it is, in fact, a contributor to our inner peace, compassion, and compassion for the world around us. Whether it be in the monasteries, the mosques, the temples or in the privacy of one's own home, spiritual minimalism teaches us how to live a life steeped in self-awareness, thanksgiving, and a healthy respect for the sanctity of life.

In so far as we choose the sanctified way of simple life, we are not just maneuvering our physical lives, but commencing inner transformation - a spiritual journey. It is a path that incites us to be selective by shedding the outer crusts and tuning in to the core that is life.

It is a journey that calls us to lose all non-essentials, to stay focused on what matters and to be calm in the quiet and clearness one gets by living with control and goal. From here, we collect that minimalism is not something one does—it is a way of being, a terrific example of our spiritual values, and our most loved connection with the divine.

Finding Serenity in the City

Urban living, with its never-ending life and pace, comes with special difficulties for those who want to have less stuff so they can live a minimalist life. Space shortages, high living costs, and the constant urban noises are hard to avoid and might give us the impression that simplicity is inaccessible. However, urban minimalism is not only possible, but also it is a completely attractive and productive way of dealing with the charming chaos. Urbanites can take advantage of minimalist principles to establish a well-polished and peaceful lifestyle among the crowded city streets.

One of the most urgent battles for urban minimalists the scarcity of space. Urban apartments and houses are always much more confined than the ones in suburban or rural areas, thus, people have to decide what belongings they will really need. As such, every inch of the living quarters is accounted for and the minimalists of urban areas often resort to the adoption of unusual strategies to make the most of their surroundings. Multi-functional furniture such as, for example, pull-down beds, tables that both serve as desks, and storage ottomans are items that a frequently sighted in the urban minimalism environment. In practice, not only do they conserve the much-needed space, they also help in cutting down the number of multiple items needed, which in turn contributes to a more efficient and uncluttered room.

In addition to the physical, mental and emotional space is also in short supply for city residents. City life induces a continuous push-stimulus through the noise, crowd, advertising and regular movements that involve the street traffic. Urban minimalism is the solution that aims at simply the elimination of the sensory stress in addition to the physical one. This should be exemplified by the presence of one quiet and serene space in a home which a resident can visit away from the city noise, or practicing digital minimalism to minimize the mental baggage of continuous cyber links and information load.

One of the closest correlation between digital minimalism and urban areas is noticeable in the fact that these areas are flooded with work, social life, and technology in most cases. Continued connection in cities is a reason for utmost pressure. Being at a place like a city with the need to keep in touch by emails, social media such as Facebook, Twitter, and Myspace, and messenger applications like Telegram Slip is very often suffocating. Uzbekistans of cities tend to create solutions to the ever-growing digital mess. These may involve clocks to turn on or off the screens according to the time limits, a selection of those sites which are full of concrete forums for chatting with strangers, and the last one is about the performance of factories which are "locked" for a number of hours. In contrast, digital devices can be put in "unlock" mode. And entail hideaway

Another of the most basic aspects of urban minimalism is being mindful in consumption. In the arenas of cities, where consumption is at the mouth of people—from coffee shops and restaurants to shops and advertisements at virtually any corner of the street—the main alternative left is to become adept in mindful consumption. Urban minimalists do not just take whatever they are offered to buy but rather they make beneficial choices like focusing on the quality, quantity, and impact that the items bought on the environment and society carry. This is where one can see the connection with local eco-enterprises or choosing pre-owned or renewable products. In the same vein, not buying unnecessary things and rather prioritizing purchases that add value to one's life, is a way of consuming mindfully.

Not all cases of minimalism in city areas are entirely as a result of adopting the austerity lifestyle. In reality, urban minimalism is one of the unavoidable ways of life for certain people who cannot afford a more extravagant one. Besides being a lavish place to live, the upkeep costs in urban parts can be an instrument of minimalization of one's life. The reason behind such people's decisions is usually that their income is being squandered for rent and survival. Thus, people of the urban community tend to live with fewer possessions as a form of money and stress reduction. This situation can be addressed in various strategies including shrinking the current living space, sharing the housing space with others, or else following the main principles of the tiny house movement where fewer resources are used and waste amount is reduced.

Urban minimalism is embodies in the tiny house movement, which has made through their way into numerous urban areas. These little, oftentimes movable residential units are designed to maximally exploit space as well as reducing the environmental effect. For the people living in overcrowded parts of a city, so-called tiny houses offer an alternative which does not just the realization of an opportunity to l..., but also to an environmentally friendly way of life. The movement in this respect also aligns with the minimalist goals of being content with what is enough and avoid the rest. In cities where the population is too high, and space is a scarce resource, this movement has become more common and demonstrated the usefulness as well as the right way of having a full life with less stress.

This is another share-d living concept, an emerging life-style in city simplicity. In doing so, communal living benefit its re-sidents. It encourages things like-gender equality, loyalty, compliance-, compassion, and teamwork. This comes in the form of funding a coope-rative project. In such setups, the-residents are the- only owners and exclusive me-mbers of the operation. At the- same time, reside-nts may join forces to handle various parts of the dwe-lling, such as meals, cleaning, or lawn maintenance-. This sort of space becomes a habitat for promoting a tight-knit community fe-eling. In fact, the societal and e-nvironmental exchanges re-sulting from this are...."

One of the ways that urban minimalism is intertwined with the enormous trend of sustainability in cities. The reality is that urban minimalists reflect the individual need for social responsibility by seeking to cut their energy consumption needs, acknowledging the fact that metropolitan areas produce more waste than any other place and it remains very important. Through practising simplicity, urban minimalists' declining consumption and advocating for sustainable practices, they act like an institution in the form of such cities. Choosing to walk or cycle is one of the options to assist with the reduction of CO2 emissions; instead of using energy, designing transit (Zukin, 2008). However, this does not prove adequate in solving the "wicked problem" of urban environmental degradation.

The challenges of urban minimalism are not only inherited because of the built environment but they can also be a result of habits from the overly consuming society and limited space. Nevertheless, the challenges that urban life brings can turn into opportunities for urban dwellers to come up with innovative solutions. One of the things that get the attention of the DOE office of Energy Efficiency and Renewable Energy is to adopt minimalism by creating multifunctional housing that depends on small instead of large-scale investments in energy-saving materials. Other projects are mirroring sustainability such as the VELUX project Urban Living in the Sustainable City. Its residents practice car sharing and live in solar-powered homes. Smart Gardens are another nature-based design concept the students have tried that can also offer alternative green spaces other than leisure activities.

Urban dwellers embrace minimalism not because they had to but because it can be a more appealing and a welcome tonic to the fast-paced, overwhelming chaos. City people can find peace and mindfulness in the city by consuming fewer and opting for an eco-friendly urban lifestyle. This method is not only beneficial to the individual; it also helps to cultivate an environment that is richer in terms of sustainable, environmental, and community benefits.

Urban minimalism, in its essence, is a result of human sensitivity to the environment of a city. It is a principle that looks at the problems in urban development and answers them with reasonable solutions. If not in the design of housing, it may also be in the conversations on the amount of trash to be removed from their location, or even in curbing consumerism. Self-sustaining townships act as the solution to the issue of fast urbanization where the population exceeds the available resources that the city can provide. Resham strives to achieve sustainability while sustaining the cultural integrity of the city all winter.

In the overwhelming urban milieu, where time, space, and resource consumption become super-burdens, urban minimalism is an opportunity to step toward a balanced and meaningful life. Minimalism focuses on the core of essential things and encourages the individuals to appreciate what they truly need. Thus, the whole communities are also gaining from the developments as cities grow to be a bit healthier, more alive, and in harmony.

The Wisdom of Simple Living

The minimalist movement is a response that emerged not because of ordinary folks, mostly. It was the result of the overwhelming demands of consumerism and material excess. However, the principles of minimalism—simplicity, self-sufficiency, and a deep connection to nature—are not new. They have been represented in the rural and traditional lifestyle of agrarian societies and in the indigenous communities of the whole world. These people have followed a type of minimalism, which combines practical and spiritual aspects. It is based on a profound reverence for the natural world and a close connection to the very principle of life itself, living within its limits.

Simple lifestyle in rural and traditional societies has always been practical matters and not because it is fashionable. "Enough" is Be it that the communities see the limitation. Resources are often limited, and the imperative to live in harmony directly with nature requires frugality, resourcefulness, and a deep understanding of the environment. The rural mindset and the desire to do minimalism are rather than those devoted to modern minimalistic movements. Rural minimalism comprises techniques where no unnecessary use of resources is made and every aspect of life is made sustainable.

One of the main components of rural and traditional minimalism is self-sufficiency. In agrarian societies, individuals who are able to provide for their own needs as well as their families without being too dependent on any outside sources are the basic members of the community. Apart from the part when one wants to grow his food or the one wear his clothes, it means more for him the whole philosophy of independent and resilient. The practicalities needed to survive, such as, farming, animal husbandry, and craftsmanship, all of them are passed down through the generations, and they include methods for sustainable living.

Many rural and indigenous societies are not only engaged in resourcefulness but are also minimalistic in the classical manner. Waste-free practices dictate societal life in these societies. Each and every thing is reutilized, each and every thing is utilized to the maxim, and the use and reuse process is the indispensable part of the daily routine. For instance, in the context of such populations, there the raw materials for clothing, tools, and shelter are derived directly from nature, and of course they are utilized conscientiously. The skins of the animals are turned into clothing, the bones are formed into the tools, and every single part of the plant is used in some way. This carrying out principle has, for one thing, waste reduction as a goal but it is also a counteraction to environmental degradation since people all the time have a visual and physical presence in their relationships with nature and feel their bond with the world.

Hence, sustainability is not just a trendy word in these areas but a cultural commitment. The indigenous practices of hunting, building, and farming are all about staying one with nature and thus making it not less rich in resources and more fertile for next generations. There are numerous indigenous societies that show a great deal of stewardship where the land is not seen as a commodity to be exploited but as an entity that needs to be taken care of. This understanding of fair use has become part of the very culture and spirituality: from ceremonies to daily habits.

The sparse principles of the countryside and the ancient ways also serve as a spiritual aspect. In a good lot of them, simplicity, to be quite honest, is not just a matter of the immediate need for practical reason, but actually it is a spiritual end that has to be achieved. One recognizes the fact that material possessions and wealth do not bring happiness or satisfaction, and that inner peace is what causes man to live in unity with nature, forge relations with other humans, and keep to spiritual and moral principles. An exemplification of such teachings is found in many indigenous religions, which stand for humility, gratitude, and adaptation of one's behavior to the environment.

The lifestyle in traditional societies is so different from the affluent consumerist capitalist way of life rampant in most modern countries today, where wealth and the accumulation of material things are often regarded as synonymous with success in life. In rural and traditional communities, the major concept of life is to live a good and essential life — a life that is simple, balanced, and that is close to nature and people. Such a spartan lifestyle confronts the deeply ingrained cultural belief that more is better, and instead argues that less could be more provided it comes along with a sense of purpose, meaning, and a feeling of belonging the community.

New-age minimalists cansource a lot from the rural and traditional lifestyle. The severe environmental conditions, strong resource consciousness, and symbiotic relations that rural Earthmen have observed provide substantial insights for people who want to live a more mindful and environmentally friendly life. By following strategies such as growing their own food, producing less waste, and putting quality over quantity, modern minimalists can change their ways to become more inline with historical societal values.

Additionally, the spiritual side of the rural minimalism phenomenon gives the modern minimalist movement a more in-depth perspective. The notion that joy and satisfaction are not achieved through material things but rather through connections – to the Earth, to the people around you, and to the higher power – can be a very valuable improvement for the minimalist philosophy and its practice. The spiritual dimension can uplift the minimalist way of living beyond the externality of decluttering into a more rounded approach to simplicity.

There are other lessons that one should draw from the public aspects of typical minimalism. In a lot of rural communities, the community's welfare always comes before the individual's wants, and the resources are spread among all to ensure that they are provided with what they need. Indeed, the sense of community and the mutual support are the things of the past, as they are these days lacking in modern cities where the individualism of the population and the outrageous competition for scarce resources have become the norm. Through the development of community sense and prioritizing collective well-being though, modern minimalists can create cohesive social networks that would comply with the practices based on the principle of shared living which exists in both urban and rural settings.

However, there are also some points that need to be considered in the course of integration of these traditional practices, namely the approach has to be respectful and humble. Rural and indigenous wisdom should not be treated as merchandise and incorrectly linked to it but be acknowledged for its profundity and weight. In this way, modern minimalists can grow in their practice while taking a twofold approach that does not infringe on the cultural and historical landscapes of their emergence.

By investigating the overlap of rural and traditional practices with the minimalism concept, it is evident that the core principles of simplicity, sustainability, and self-reliance were already in existence long ago. Indeed, these practices affirm the notion that living without waste is a more conscious companion to present leeway but is a timeless practice of life that had supported communities and cultures for centuries.

Like the new minimalism school, it copies the rural folk ways, the evolution of the new minimalism by drawing inspiration from the traditional societies and the communities of the past to come up with provisions that cater for all residents in urban areas by making people learn to live without many resources and respecting nature. The wisdom of rural and traditional minimalism reminds us that our lives will be more fulfilling if we reduce our possessions and, in their place, incorporate meaningful living and intention into our lives. They offer a stark reflection of nature that goes beyond mere materialism.

Minimalism and the Fabric of Society

Minimalism, is often seen as a personal or lifestyle choice and having an influence on the social structures that constrain it also is quite meaningful. It is the approach whereby minimalism, being a definer of simple things, leading a deliberate lifestyle and reducing excess, not only interacts with these but also affects the family dynamics, collective living, social hierarchy and cultural norms. By investigating the mixed up issues of simplicity and social life, we will get the answer of this puzzle. Will it be using minimalism to strengthen social justice issues or will it only just be changed to create more inequity and exclusivity. These are the questions we need to tackle.

Family, which involves a child-parent or spouse relationship, is the core of most of the social structures that vary from the size, responsibilities, and roles of the family in different cultures. The practice of minimalism that involves simpler, more meaningful living through being content with fewer possessions can help a lot of families by changing the way family members act and interact. In contrast, if the family has a collectivistic orientation, which to a great extent comes from the fact that a person is deeply connected to the family of origin and this family serves as a basis for an identity, minimalism's ideas of overcoming the traditional beliefs of the necessity of financial wealth might hierarchic the social life right. Usually, in these communities, however, people sit on Mount Olympus on account of their still eternally soaring fortunes. Owning imported cars, sturdy buildings and other assets are the means to show off in the extended family and to maintain high esteem in society. Here, it is minimalism that gives a new and better definition of true wealth, which is not about having more money but involves having more and better relationships among people and experiences that count.

In these settings, simplicity can act as a starting point for redefining success and ranking in terms of popularity. Instead of consumerism as a way to family obligations, minimalists in collectivistic cultures might argue the significance of common experiences, the community's help, and the health of all the members in the family. This new direction in finding the balance of needs in the family unit can lead to the family using fewer resources, not tied to the concept of materialism, and experiencing contentment and joy that arises independent of wealth.

In Western cultures, where the characteristics of freedom and individualism are cultivated among the population, minimalism often blends in well with the existing social norms. The essence of less consumerism and thus living life more intentionally, fits in quite smoothly with the individualistic ideology of making choices freely and taking charge over one's own life. Even though the process of minimalism can be complicated within these societies, it can challenge the culture of consumption domination and the status pursuit through material accumulation. People who prefer intentional and mindful consumption over just going for more and more stuff in these societies are the very kind of minimalists which the society boasts

Moreover, a minimalist approach can entice new social hierarchies to emerge by questioning the traditional status and success symbols. The emphasis on the material possessions as a marker of social success is widespread and often more the ones that have a lot are seen as more successful or significant than others. This materialistic mindset that is prevalent in the society frequently gives rise to social discrimination as it is an idea that the individual's value is attached to what they possess rather than what their personality is like and their contributions to society. Contrarily, minimalism presents a point of view that is built upon the values of simplicity, honesty, and the pursuit of a meaningful life over the acquisition of worldly goods. Thereby minimalists may inspire others, as well, to revolt the traditional function of coins, by initiating debates about other notions of success, say such as personal developments, creativity, or community contribution.

While the distribution of resources and opportunities is unevenly distributed across various cultures, each one has its own set of privileges and power commodities. Societies can use minimalism—which is a means to learn to live with less and commit oneself to a single purpose—to promote a more just use of resources and to move from the often harmful materialistic values that are the main causes of social inequalities. For example, umbrageous, environmentally friendly manufactures and consumers might argue that minimalism is an overriding dogma for sustainability whose ambition is to be fair to others while solving the social and ecological impacts of our actions at the local and global levels. With such an approach, the society can be characterised by more justice and its inclusivity would be achieved at the expense of personal progress.

In addition to this, the essence of minimalism goes beyond the common consumerist narratives to express the importance of more engaged and connected communities through limited consumption. In the ultra-modern west communal life is buried under the avalanche of hyper-individualism and hyper-consumption. Traditional society affirms that the majority's cooperation is the only recipe for success. Minimalism can be the remedy creating space for social values that don't center on material things and, in fact, allow mutual help and support. This could mean sharing resources, volunteering for community projects, or merely loving others more than can be achieved with the acquisition of material goods. By adopting the principles of minimalism, communities can build strong relationships and with that, social ties will prevail above individual manifestations thus, leading to collective success.

Despite this, minimalism becomes a reality in our social cues as it is deprived of the followership of becoming a way of life. That is, more than the materialistic culture, people often have their personal identity and self-worth derived from the wealth they own. While minimalists are viewed on a personal level, to some, society takes it as an offense from their part for not acknowledging their sincere efforts and accomplishments. In my view, this may take the form of cultural rejection where some minimalist styles are not only questioned but some may even go so far as to call it a cultural betrayal. It leads them to look for a solution to the problem which could be to look for other solutions or even other ways of living.

Overcoming the resistance or ignorance of the other constituents of society, minimalists are themselves a part of, and particularly their families, is necessary. Yet if a minimalist practice is regarded as opposed to traditional commitments of family provision or community participation, tensions may emerge within families or neighborhoods, the study finds. By minimizing expenses and aspects of financial stress that are not crucial or by participating in invested venture funds, minimalists will produce a family fund that is jointly organized.

The seven Marys who attained self-actualization as minimalists symbolize growing into empowering minimalistic life, even when expenses might be irrelevant. Particularly whereas gathering people to the community is not a materially manifested action, it may be rather a project to be interested in. This is not something to be forced upon them as this could lead them to understand differently the approach.

There are also ways in which such a phenomenon called minimalism can be modified to be incompatible with different cultural frameworks and yet remain to be negligible. To this end, minimalism could be formed as a manner of living in particularly tight cultural and social contexts through which one could process life with the basic standard irrespective of any particular cultural constraints. An example of this would be to use safe eco-friendly means of transport to the workplace which are also easy on the pocket for the investors.

A minimalism, that is, minimalist practice has both, a capability to subvert and bolster the established social institutions, while such variety of practices and readings are found when minimalism is in different cultural contexts. Through the questioning of the correlation of material wealth to the notion of success and status, minimalists can be of help in leading the community to a redefined and more just version of the good life. This means the society will be able to establish some principles like relationships, well-being, and sustainability as its priority focus over the accumulation of possessions.

So, modern minimalism that is becoming more and more popular globally requires us to look at it from the socio-political prisms in which it is practiced. Minimalism becomes a transformational model through which people in collectivist or individualistic cultures, in well-off or poor communities can rediscover the value of relationships as the mainstay of the society and shift their attention to what really counts. If we habituate the principles guiding a minimalist lifestyle to diversely woven cultural frames, we can attain a fairer order with human beings at the center and where the criteria not the owning of wealth but a good life lived become the measure of success.

Minimalism's Global Wave

Minimalism, one time, a niche lifestyle, has become a worldwide trend that is favored by people everywhere, despite their different cultures and backgrounds. Among others, its rise can be attributable to some factors, such as the influence of globalisation, the growing impact of digital technology on our daily lives, and the surge of environmental concerns around the globe. As it unfolds across countries, not only the West but minimalism is to be considered from cultural variation points of view or the intermediation of the movement, lets, therefore raise questions as to its acceptance in the global cultural sphere and its signification among other locations.

The contemporary history of the minimalist movement can be connected to several different cultural streams. In the West, Minimalism has often been juxtaposed with the "less is more" philosophy that originally took shape in the 1940s, mainly in the areas of architecture and design. The minimalist look, characterized by clean lines, open or negative spaces and a reduction of clutter, has infiltrated several segments of the western society, i.e. interior design and in the lifestyle choices of the people. This fashion, which is more than beautiful to the eye, is a cultural change towards simplicity and intentionality as it stands an accusation for our blind run after the wealth that we clutter our things with.

One of Europe's most minimalist regional aesthetics would definitely be that of Scandinavia. There, the concept of "lagom" which stands for "the perfect balance" has been guiding the people for decades. The Scandinavian minimalist style is not just about aesthetics; its main features could be tracked back to the cultural mindset that thinks over balance, sustainability, and connection to the environment. Minimalism in Scandinavia is always focused on the essential and the beautiful and it promotes a lifestyle that is not only nature-friendly but also satisfyingly holistic. This achievements in the regional segment have been instrumental in shaping the entire design world alongside convincing many of us to opt for the path of a less-consumption-life.

The minimalistic theme had been popular in Japan for many years in traditional and modern variants. Zen Buddhism, a spiritual philosophy of simplicity, mindfulness, and the elimination of distractions, which is rooted in the Japanese tradition, has been heavily influenced by the minimalist trend. A spiritual aspect of minimalism can be observed in the Japanese tea ceremony, architecture, and even in the art of flower arranging, which is wherein the simplicity and intention are the most significant. In the recent years, Japan, also along with the global minimalist movement, has been brought thanks to people like Marie Kondo, whose KonMari method has become worldwide practice. Kondo is celebrating the approach to decluttering which suggests to people to hold their possessions that bring happiness or "spark joy," the message of which has been equivalent in the global community through different cultures, to that of the KonMari method which offers an easy and emotional solution to living a minimalist life.

The expansion of minimalism all around the world has been driven by the factors of globalization and digital communications. In a world that is becoming more interconnected, the easy and fast sharing and adoption of ideas and trends took place. Social platforms like social media, blogs, and online communities have greatly contributed to the increase of minimalism within the mainstream, thus giving everyone a chance to learn and share their stories about it. The era of technology has given birth to "digital minimalism" — a lifestyle in which people minimize their exposure to technology by limiting screen time, shaping their digital living spaces, and concentrating on quality social interactions.

Minimalism is reaching worldwide due not only to the fact that the population as a whole has come to realize the brevity of earthly resources though our planet is just one. As people have been taught about the natural disasters and environmental pollution, a portion of them began minimalism with the view to the decrease in the polluting of nature. The whole idea of minimalism that is based on living with fewer materials, spending wisely and taking care of the environment, which has been promoted through the environmental movement, links strongly with their objectives. Thus, minimalism has a more significant role in the world as it is seen as a global phenomenon and even the young generation will also benefit from it.

Even though it became the object of attention on a global scale, minimalism should not be overlooked by its detractors and shortcomings. One of the critical negative opinions is the fact that minimalism is sometimes encountered as the privilege of the people who already have enough and so it cannot be approached by others. People struggling to make ends meet might have difficulty grappling with the idea of living on concepts such as reducing the number of possessions or simplifying lifestyles because, in their opinion, they are already out of reach or pointless. This critique underlines the importance of the minimalist movement to cater for the diverse realities of human lives; the movement should be more inclusive to be able to do that. We must change minimalism so that it becomes not only the behavior that the more prosperous adopt but a way of thinking that can be suited for all conditions.

Commodification is one of the most difficult aspects of minimalism. It becomes a problem because minimalism indeed becomes a trend and companies and brands can earn money by selling those things. This paradoxically means that the companies and stores that market such goods as absolutely necessary for a minimalistic lifestyle actually undermine the very principles of simplicity and mindful consumption. To stay true to its mission, the minimalist movement has to prevent the spread of commercialization and concentrate on key elements, namely living with intention and creating less waste.

One of the cultural adaptations that is actually central to the spread of minimalism around the world, is the idea that minimalism's core principles — simplicity, intentionality, and sustainability (to name a few) — are universal, while the differences in the way different cultures and societies practice them are very large. A good example of it could be the fact that the collectivist cultures where solicitous family and community ties are present minimalism might be oriented more towards promoting the collective well-being of all and sharing the resources instead of personal decluttering. By contrast, minimalism in the other i.e. individualistic societies may be centered around the concepts of self-determination, autonomy, and the feat of a more deliberate lifestyle on an individual basis. Needless to say, the recognition and respect of these differences, the understanding of these cultural differences is the key point in the non-stop process of the minimalist movement.

In order to be truly universal and inclusive it is evident that in addition to environmental sustainability, the minimalist movement has to focus on social equity and justice. Minimalism should not be a means of filtering out these issues but rather a method of confronting and challenging them. Through the promotion of ecological sustainability, fair trade, consumption of non-toxic products, and a downsizing of the focus on material wealth minimalism can help in building a more egalitarian society where resources are shared more justly and the focus is on common good instead of individual acquisition.

It is quite obvious when investigating the emergence of minimalism as a global movement that this lifestyle actually appeals to people of other countries for different reasons. On a global scale, many people have been inspired to adopt this lifestyle that promotes simplicity by its ecologically responsible approach. People may be driven into embracing minimalism because of the growing environmental issues, a wish for simplicity, or proper rejection of consumer culture. To not homogenize the idea of minimalism and for people to avoid giving up their unique cultural values while the spread of minimalism continues will curb the appropriation of meaningful change in people's lives and the society at large.

For minimalism to attain global status it is a must that this approach upon which it is based will be able to adapt and be inclusive to all cultures and their conditions. By so doing it will be able to continue getting people to be more intentional, greener and more meaningful and thus create a healthier and balanced world. Simplicity, intentionality and sustainability are the central values given across the whole world. The world is not divided because of the true values but because of the non-existence of fair politics. Simplicity shows us how much connected and related the world and culture are and what is it that people collectively want. We must be straightforward and act this way in a moment when our kids' future is being decided and the direction is totally wrong

In the end, the global movement of minimalism is not just about reducing what we have but about rethinking what we value and how we live. It goes beyond and makes us look at what we really treasure in life and how we can choose to participate accordingly. As the philosophy of minimalism proceeds with the intermixing of different cultures, it provokes reflection of the fact that simplicity is an outcome that is beyond territories and it is also alive in every human who craves a life of truth and dedication.

Chapter 8

Overcoming Barriers to Minimalism

The word denomination refers to an approach that requires a person to let go of the things that are not necessary in life and to become more attentive to the little things that are unique. A minimalist philosophy rests on the promise of simplicity and its associated properties, such as clarity and the attention that is afforded to essential things. Minimalism's focus on immediate needs and avoiding the negatives of today's consumer culture is one of the most engaging aspects of this way of life. The idea of minimalism, meaning less stuff, more profound interactions, and the desire to gain knowledge and new experiences, has gained appreciation from people all around the world. However, even though the principles of minimalism might seem plain, the process of becoming this way of life is often entangled with obstacles. The minimalistic path includes not only the act of decluttering and reducing the number of possessions one has, but it also entails confronting ingrained mental habits, social pattern, emotional, and personal attachments which can make the transition itself a real challenge. In this chapter, we look into the issues that act as barriers to minimalism and provide solutions to get over them.

The pressure of meeting people's expectations is one of the symptoms of social anxiety. People sometimes do what the other people do so as to be able to follow the ones they know, or those close to them, even if that implies their lives have to be more complex which is contrary to their wish for a simpler. But the fear of being rejected or misunderstood for one's choice of a different way of life is a major impediment to the adoption of minimalism. To weaken this obstacle, it is vital to first shape a set of values for oneself and then establish these principles in the minimalization that one wants to achieve. One of the fulcrums of living a minimalistic life is the ability to clearly distinguish between the things that provide the real meaning of life and the fake one that scales you over material collection. For instance, we can prioritize our desires for more leisure time, freedom, or peace by developing a deep understanding of the fact that they are the most career-defining goals which we may pursue.

Our emotional attachment to property is another obstacle which many people find challenging to be the believers of minimalism. Things such as family heirlooms or possessions that symbolize famous memories, relationships, and personages. Getting rid of such pieces may feel like a part of its power, however, should we as well be prone to negative feelings and bereavement. This sentiment can discourage the attempt of the cleaning process that one engages in as we struggle to differentiate the emotional value from the physical one.

Firstly, digging into the roots of these affections to comprehend them better is critical. We need to understand that while objects can remind us of our memories, they are not the memories themselves. We own the sentimental items and we are the ones who will carry on the legacy of the sentimentality through the objects. By minimizing our attention on the objects that are already with us, we can start forgiving ourselves with more comfort. Besides, there are some practical solutions that can help right away, for instance, taking photos or selecting some of the most precious items, which also will make the process easier. Emotional sentiment is not necessarily the only thing that is required to love an item; the main aim should be to comprise the things that add strength to your journey and are in line with your latest values. The purpose is not to burn all the memories along with the connection but to pick a few of them that are genuinely of great enjoyment to go along only.

The FOMO or fear of missing out is one of the most common barriers that people face in the journey to a minimalist lifestyle. There are so many opportunities, experiences, and things that are today promoted as new and better, admired, or even wretched that literally one can get lost. The acting program in complexity theory showed that the Company H could change for good. The FOMO can compel us to accumulate more stuff, engage in more activities, or go after certain ways of life because of the fear of not having what we want or need. Minimalism is a way of life that truly represents the power of less in that it asks us to consider our purchases by need or functionality and how we can reuse, repair, borrow, or trade without throwing away the old item.

In order to show the full beauty of the own treasure house, one must first be willing to see through the illusion of comparative wealth. The relinquishing of the belief that less is equal to having less than we deserve, and therefore, we ought to have more of something is an essential prerequisite to our true state of freedom. By bringing gratitude into what is present, and by changing what we would call fulfillment and joy in our life, through which we would not be exposed to any peril, the wave of anxiety that terrifies us would be let go. Minimalism, from which we derive challenging questions and dilemmas, points out the importance of efficient usage and careful selection of all bought stuff, revolutionary idea of which encourages to more for less and the satisfaction that comes with both collective good and individual fulfillment.

Supporting inner power to develop and grow is another fear that lots of people experience while they are in the way to becoming a minimalist. The excitement at the start of the process of getting rid of the clutter and making things simple can wear off as the week progresses and space gets filled with new, yet similarly time-consuming, requirements. In a society that encourages buying and wanting new items, it is hard to be firm believers in minimalism. This is where the importance of reflection and reassessment comes in. By rethinking our core values, objectives, and even the comprehensive grounds of our adoption of this lifestyle, we can rededicate ourselves to living in a simple and spartan way. Being connected to the minimalist community can also be a powerful method for maintaining the minimalist attitude. Connecting with other minimalist groups of people, checking out new books, movies, or documentaries on the topic, all can be some of the alternatives that might be used to get or regain the minimalism insights.

Avoiding everything, we need to be aware that minimalism is a process, not a one-off action. It's about choosing what connects or supports our aspirations and brings us closer to our mental health. New activities could arise, such as "no-buy" or a digital detox, which we can use to enforce our effort to lead simple life. Another reason for minimalism is to praise the healthy effects on the mind and body like reducing the stress, getting clarity and gaining more freedom. All these acts are so powerful and they make you believe that this is the real way to go.

In closure, removing noise has a profound effect on the individual however; it may not be possible without the support of the family members and the demand to mend the relationship rifts. Different thoughts about what to own, and what to buy can lead to trouble and misunderstandings between family members, and thereby sustain minimalism becomes immensely difficult. It so very much depends on conversations and on finding a solution. Must react to these encounters with pity and consideration, knowing minimalism approaches might vary a lot from a person to another. Not only will we show that minimalism is beneficial but by our own living example, we can encourage others to try out living simply.

Not only that but also the practice of minimalism usually involves tackling the dynamics existing between family members and friends. Being at different levels of consumerism can cause tension or fighting between family members and therefore keeping the life of minimalism can be tricky. Communication skills are vital, and common interests need to be found or agreed upon. It's important to take a caring and empathetic approach when engaging in these interactions, which is true even though everyone is living and experiencing minimalism in different ways. However, if we inspire others by living the way we expect them to with proof of the goodness and benefits of minimalism as given by our own stories, it will work.

Battling minimalism insecurities implies that you must be patient, persistent and highly dedicated to the virtues that guide this lifestyle. And the benefits can be so diverse that the journey, despite the obstacles, becomes worthwhile. By facing the challenges and pushing through them, we will construct a life that is both simple and graced with meaning, kinship, and satisfaction. In the behind sections, we take a closer look at each barrier and come up with practical ways to use them to help you learn the way of minimalism easily and unambiguously.

Resisting the Call of Consumerism

Modern societies have a real problem regarding the role of consumption in the definition of the self, the meaning of existence, and the most effective ways for people to achieve happiness and fulfillment. From the time we turn off the alarm the morning until the time we put our heads on pillows the consumerist messages of the media are ceaselessly overbearing. Advertising, social networks, or the expectations of people around us can reinforce the ideas that the possessions we own are directly connected to our happiness and success in life. Living in this environment makes it a very difficult task to endorse the ideological values or lifestyle of minimalism. Which can probably be seen as a specific way of being that promotes the rejection of excess and consumerism in favor of living life in simplicity, intentionality, and contemplation.

Consumerist culture persuades individuals that they can achieve true happiness only by acquiring objects of desire. Advertisements make people desire certain goods that promise to add value to their lives like for instance that latest smartphone, fashionable attire, or an expensive car. The mesmerized consumers by presenting them as the evidence of the ultimate aim of human fulfillment or the desired person image. It looks like social networks to an even larger extent enhance these fake and unnatural models for behavior as millions of users post images of their glossy and seemingly perfect properties and lives. The effect of these insinuating adverts creates an atmosphere of constant comparison and dissatisfaction, with many people basing their self-worth on their possessions. The fight to represent a certain brand lifestyle and syndrome of FOMO brought about by every single post from the Kardashian or your high school classmate may seem unending as . people bombard you with this fear of missing out.

However, the truth is that happiness that stems from consumption is lives of people can be qualitatively characterized as empty and internally empty. Even though newly acquired items can grant us the fleeting pleasure and feeling of fulfillment, this feeling tends to be ephemeral, short-lived, and unsustainable. Within a few days after bringing home an unexpected item, this substance, which is charming at first, stops to cause excitement again and becomes just another object. Nevertheless, people distract themselves from the realization of emptiness inside themselves by buying certain products and wait for the next buying to happen. In such a cycle of need and letdown, people find themselves in a dead-end, where satisfaction can be achieved through consumerism, but never acquired. The problem is not that more things are good, but that no thing will ever be enough or even truly satisfying for an individual trying to fill an empty place achieved by the fall of the illusion of consumerism.

In order to effectively resist the pervasive force of consumer culture that continues to surround us, it is ever so important to develop and nurture the sense of personal values that remains disconnected from the trappings of material acquisition and wealth. This approach requires a period of profound reflection upon ourselves, thus leading to an unambiguous understanding of what Western society terms as the right and the important things in life. Some people hold the belief that the bonds of relationships, the phenomena of personal development, or the culturally enriching experiences responsible for personal joy and fulfillment are what counts as important in life. In the same vein, some people see as an important point a strong commitment to the principles of sustainability, environmental protection, or the community of believers. In essence, no matter what these personal core values are, having a generally solid and durable foundation of values can go a long way in helping individuals to resist the almost irresistible temptation to blindly buy into the consumerist mindset.

Yet another effective strategy for holding onto a minimalist mindset amidst the societal pressures to consume is the backup of clearly and specifically defined goals based on these very values. Having developed a vision of the kind of life that is in congruence with the philosophies of minimalism, one is able to see a life where meaning, sense of purpose, and wellbeing supersede the factors of material abundance. Therefore, making the types of decisions that fit within this scope becomes an easier process for the decision-making process. Rather than acting like a mere compass, these goals act as a filter through a range of choices that individually face us in the passage of each new day. Be it her choice to channel her financial resources into creating experiences vested with eternal value as opposed to buying temporary pleasure in the material items, or whether the decision to abstain from a social event not in accordance with the values; these clearly defined goals have the power and capacity to keep individuals on the desired path that leads to minimalism.

Finally, the final component of the resistance against social pressure in light of consumerism implies mindful consumption as a practice where the consumptive decisions are made in an active, conscious, and engaging manner. Mindfulness here means being aware of the need, cognition, and the framework within which the given product intersects with our previous beliefs concerning the values and specific objectives. Accordingly, it implies asking ourselves the critical questions that pave the way to reasonable decisions prior to stating the purchasing intention: Do I really need this? Is there a possibility that this purchase will ever truly be of value and joy in my life? Is this purchase aligned with the kind of life I want to lead? The practice of mindful consumption encourages us to free ourselves from our automatic behaviours that often lead to unnecessary accumulation and shifts the focus of our attention onto purposeful consumption that has a positive impact on our lives. As a result, by integrating these practices into our everyday lives, we begin building a more balanced relationship with ourselves, thus empowering us to live according to our core values and shaping our reality as opposed to being shaped by it.

In the process of developing an intrinsic sense of value towards some things in life such as possessions, one can work on enhancing the way they consume things through simplicity. This can be achieved through the social concept of simplicity whereby one would have a group of people who share similar minimalist ideologies such that they would uplift one another in the practices of efficient consumption. One can say that such support groups play an important role in shaping how people perceive and act towards certain issues and by being in company with individuals with a lifestyle that focuses on minimal living the insights can be advantageous and do away with unnecessary ignorance, which interferes with practices that simplify and give value to life. Whether you are in search of like-minded people by means of physical meetings, online forums or connecting with engaged friends who are already in this lifestyle, looking for motivation and at the same time giving it back can hugely facilitate and additionally increase the satisfaction of going for an easier way to the existence based on lets say the' essentials' especially. This group could also offer significant help in the form of advice with respect to the minor details and occurrences that pass for minimalistic living, strengthening their strong commitment and reflecting on the reason of their choice of minimalist living in its realistic sense and confirming these ideals indeed manifest in the daily activities.

Another crucial step in living a minimalistic life is the ability to navigate through all the problems and the entirety of society's pressure and aspects of consumer culture that constantly surround a person and drive him. One of the commonly shared assumptions in these societies would be that more is always better therefore success is becoming defined by the amount and quality of items that one has in their possession. Minimalism presents a different view concerning what is precious and asserts that it is not in having many things that a person can make his life successful but in living in a manner that matters. Through asking if the promises of the consumer's ground trunk are valid or actually doable in the future as well as the revelation of the terrible results that these endless purchases effects on human beings and the world that we inhabit such as the disturbing wave of climate change endangering this planet, the rats race for more, and the unending lack or inadequacy of human satisfaction, it becomes gradually evident that going for something different and lastly opting to a simpler and more responsible way of living may become a better plan in life.

It is quite essential to comprehend that the consumption in society may not only arise from the parallels that the social world presents but also from the people who exhibit real concern like family, close friends, and business partners. These individuals may express their fear about the approach or practices, and some may even suggest that the family conforms to their more conventional lifestyle and therefore in these cases, the individual may feel in some way pressured for the same. In these situations, one has to be firm in communicating our beliefs and the direction we would like to take in a manner that is not only intelligible but also without pride and does not include in it a sense of one's ideality beyond the other. By explaining to the people who care about him and sharing with them the basis behind the decision to apply minimalism in their lives a certain level of congeniality is achieved that helps others to understand the reasons as well as accept the chosen lifestyle. The important thing is that in this way, the likelihood of misunderstanding is diminished, and the chances of the others being prejudiced are also reduced which creates a better atmosphere for a minimalistic life and for acceptance of unusual choices.

For the many people out there who are finding it hard to cope with the lifestyle demands of society, it is very liberating to note that minimalism is not all about roughing it through life but rather about the total freedom that comes when one is doing the right things. For a moment and reflect well on what he has, every person has so many things that he buys just to fit in that he ends up spending more than he thought. Minimalism takes away that pressure of having to buy 'more' but instead puts the focus on the 'needed' things that are fulfilling and enjoyable in life. When people reject the need to meet the expectations associated with the status of living, they create more space for improvement and peace. Minimalism is not all about solving the problems faced by the society but rather is giving the world a chance to make the right choices. This way of living results in one living the way that he believes is right and no longer is obliged to get so much first for immediate society and secondly for the future human generations.

In standing firm against societal pressure, it emerges that minimalism can give us better choices and feelings that the material objects given by consumerism cannot give us. Presently, the temptation that comes with exposing oneself to the newest releases in terms of material possessions becomes hard to resist. The majority of the things that bring pleasure require a choice that is consistent with our ideals, do not come from the society we live in but are taken from within ourselves. If one has understood the almost hypnotizing effect that materialism has on them then they can rise above their difficulties by going through this journey of minimalism. By voluntarily choosing to bring minimalism in all aspects of their lives, people tend to acquire more. Instead of making unwanted expenditures and distributing their time and thoughts, they focus on the latter things and try to make as much sense as possible and thus gain higher achievements in the minimalism life.

In conclusion, the unfortunate truth is that societal pressure is a major spine that runs through the world of minimalism making it a difficult venture among its practitioners, but while it is difficult, it is not an impossible thing for them to adapt to it. In creating a concrete set of desire values and direction, focusing on the basic essentials, shopping with the heart and joining hands with like-minded individuals, minimalists can face the twists and turns of commercialism and stay true to their hearts. Minimalism is not so much a way to detach from society and the world, but a way to embrace the world in a manner that is true to its values. It explores the road to the real success and complete satisfaction that one can only find inside; and thus bind somebody once and for all to figure out the following. When people begin to seek purpose and fulfillment not in regards to the possessions that they have but in the persons that they are and in the living, they surely become the founders of the great future that will give birth to the great society.

Emotional Attachments to Possessions

One of the most challenging aspects of minimalism is the process of letting go of possessions that carry sentimental value. These items often hold a special place in our hearts because they are tied to important memories, relationships, or aspects of our identity. They remind us of people we love, places we've been, and experiences that have shaped who we are. As a result, the thought of parting with these possessions can evoke feelings of loss, guilt, or even fear. Yet, as we navigate the path to a simpler, more intentional life, it becomes essential to examine our emotional attachments to these items and to find ways to let go without losing what truly matters.Affixing images or thoughts to an object we own has been one of the core component factors of why we hold on to it. When we cling to possessions with sentimental value, we invest objects with personal meaning. Physical objects also serve as symbols of significant times in our lives and in this way, they freeze these moment in time. Wedding dresses, a child's first pair of shoes, special pieces of jewelry handed down through generations these objects are not merely possessions like any other they are like repositories of emotion, memory and identity. In keeping such objects, we are not merely in possession of a piece of cloth or metal; we bear or preserve the stories and feelings that are engraved on them.

This emotional investment in objects is deeply rooted in our psychology. Possessions that have sentimental value often serve as a bridge between the past and the present, helping us to maintain a connection to people and experiences that are no longer physically present in our lives. Examples of such objects include an old letter from a deceased loved one that brings back memories that make you feel close and comfortable while a souvenir from a memorable trip is similarly a portal to the joy and adventure present. These objects in a way allow us to remember moments that mattered, reinforcing our selves without, in a sense becoming attached. They are reminders of happy times that build our identity, the same part of us that is marked by the changes in time.

In conclusion, as we strive to create a minimalist lifestyle and a healthier way of living, we must be alert of the emotional and psychological ways in which we are connected to some objects. Although these belongings may anchor us to our past, it is essential to realize that we can keep the human component behind them, which is a wonderful and powerful experience. Without abandoning the objects we love, it is possible to find alternate means of capturing the most meaningful past. In the journey of minimalism and a rational and meaningful life lived, we must find the springtime of being willing to let go while maintaining the essence in those tangible. In Ninja-free and light lives, let us not be restrained by the commons of heavy uncluttered homes, but instead, let us be aside by what matters, anchors that will keep afloat in the complex ocean of life.

It is true that while we appreciate and treasure our sentimental possessions, there are indeed moments when we feel that these very same possessions weigh us down, burden us and slow us down. If we fail to curb these feelings, we may find ourselves, after accumulating more of these sentimental bits and pieces, feeling like prisoners in our own homes, encumbered by these physical reminders of the past and unable to follow the minimalist way of life that espouses the virtues of serenity and order in all things. To be sure, this almost oppressive weight of nostalgia can be compounded by the fact that the abundant and numerous sentimental items of our days may obscure the very essence of those same articles, thereby turning what were once objects of such joy and cherished memories into heaps of debris that do little else other than clutter our environment. And, thus, since we love to retain these memories and feelings that these things provide, we often reach a state where we are torn between letting go of some of these possessions and still wishing to hold on to that meaningful past that they represent and still incorporating the principles of minimalism.

The first step in solving this complicated situation has to be perhaps pretty obvious: you should not become entrapped in the notion that every bit of meaningful experience and every emotionally charged recollection that you have is described, or perhaps, symbolized, by those things. Some writers hold that these physical objects can be a memory or some other feelings they symbolize or trigger, but the most important, that is what their memory or feeling is composed of - connection, love, joy, growth, etc. Some meanings are lost when we carry around those meanings in those objects, absolutely contrary to what we might usually believe that the object must be present in order for its emotional resonance to be understood. So, by recasting the represented queries and intelligent, enthusiastic usage for the sake of creation long-held beliefs about belonging and identity within, we commenced to witness the objects stopping being objects as such, but starting to be signs of collectible memories, thus, we obtained a chance to come away from physical attachment to such souvenirs.

This perceiving change is essential to gradually detach ourselves from the emotional ties we have built around our sentimental possessions and to act in a reasoned and purposeful way when setting about the task of having any sentimental objects removed. So, instead of getting lost in such emotions as fear and guilt, which are usually evoked when one has to part with something of a counseling nature, people can professionally find out what values are being discussed without quarreling with the past that made it important and traumatic. Instead of feeling confused and frightened by a question such as, "How could I ever sell on this cherished thing?" it only remains to direct the attention at solving the problem of approaching this emotion and recollection and only the physical part of the objects that shape and embody it, and concentrate on the thought of something like, "What is the best way to celebrate or respect this cherished thought or emotion?" The stated considerations significantly expand the horizon of possible moves for disposing of the physical objects, while at the same time not detrimental to the essence of the thing. What we can do is just focus on creating a physical focus that will make significant and carry out a whole lot of different variations or manifestations when it comes to the emotion or the memory that we are associating with the object. So widely open is this course that though there may come the day that you would go ahead, sell, or discard, and still manage to hold on to that same bits of the memory, the nostalgia, and love all along the way.

One particularly useful strategy for dealing with the difficult emotions that accompany letting go of objects that have sentimental value is to take photographs of them first. With this approach we are able to encapsulate the items and capture their thingness and the feelings in them without actually retaining them physically. A photograph can elicit fond memories for when one had possession and can be stored in a digital form in a computer or printed and placed a photo album. This will not take as much space as the original item. This strategy especially comes in handy for items that have great emotional value but are hardly used or showcased like old love letters, childhood toys, and heirloom furniture. Such items mostly take up space and should one wish to keep them, one only for its good memories and not the physical thing.

Another precept that we can use to maintain our homes free from unnecessary articles where we will be when we only hold on to meaningful things is to have a select few items instead of holding on to everything. By holding a selected few that genuinely mean something to us, we can thus ensure that the items are each noticeably significant and not lost in a cluttered system of hoarding all the unnecessary things. Selecting the few items that touch us in any way can be an intense experience as we are required to be honest with ourselves on which items we truly or genuinely appreciate and which are the items that we keep because they have become a habit to have them, or some kind of debt because they were handed to us. It is like affirming and insisting that it is in the fine things that life is to be found and it is in the firm that we need to hold onto those things that create and maintain beautiful memories and connections for us.

For people who find it difficult to detach themselves from article of sentimental value, they can always look for ways of improving their function or form so that they can go on using them but in the right way. For instance, old clothes such as shirts, skirts, and long pants can be transformed into something useful such as a bed covering made up of several pieces of clothing or maybe even cushions from the same old clothes. Perhaps instead of just keeping some small items but only in a box, we should be incorporating them into a scrapbook or shadow box that can either be put on display or bee used almost every day such that they retain their value. In repurposing these cherished possessions with a new appearance or function; we can keep the good that has come with them and which we will continue to appreciate as we live a minimalist type of life.

As we go through life, we may each accumulate a number of items that have a sentimental significance. In these instances, one should keep in mind that such emotions are usually linked to the fear of forgetting or disconnecting from what rightfully belongs to the past. When we think about defensive drive to hold on to these pieces, we may fret about the possibility of losing these things may more than just losing the objects. This, however, should not stop us from having faith in our memories and making use of some alternative methods that will keep these experiences alive. With certain relatives and friends, we may want to share some anecdotes from the past, coin some thoughts into writing or establish some mythologies to commend those important people and memorable events in our lives. These acts have the potential to enrich our links to the past in a manner that would not entirely depend on belongings. It becomes feasible for us to be active participants in these memories by soaking up distinct experiences and recalling the people and things that matter the most in our lives.

Letting go of certain keepsakes is a task that calls for a level of gentleness and understanding towards ourselves. It is to be observed that emotional attachments are intricate in nature; hence it is reasonable to meet and experience different forms of emotions while having to let go of some belongings that have a significant relevance as far as feelings are concerned. It is pertinent to note that when dealing with disappointments and final farewells, we should not hurry the process; this identification hurts us, and should the need arise, for us to mourn and celebrate the times when one or another article spelt happiness or closeness is obliging so as to make sure we engage with those years and persons without having to carry along the baggage, so to speak, that may sometime inhibit us from living a complete life during this time. Minimalism is not so much about being heartless and unceremonial while relieving oneself of the most beloved things in the world but dealing with finding the sweet balance in the art of clinging on as well as setting free - of appreciating yesterday while welcoming the current)

What we try to accomplish by minimalism is not to transform our lives into empty, meaningless shells but rather to fill them up with the most vital aspects. In practicing mindful selection of which objects matter most to you on this journey that we call life, we are creating living space to breathe and to be ourselves, surrounded only by the most significant and precious items we have ever owned. This act of design has the space for liberation not only for the physical dimension but also for the emotional one and for the cognitive one, this virtue of creating the ambience in which we live and the nature of the course of our lives, of watering the spirit to grow and of taking the dirt off the soul so that it shines bright. A person can be tender to the past and yet not get bogged down by it at the same time; thus, by not allowing the past to constantly weigh them down it becomes possible for them to be in the present, and even, as one remains true to what one believes in and values with the grace of style and elegance, cautiously look to the future.

It is important to conclude that the items we choose to retain in our lives must be those that directly contribute to our well-being presently such items initiate happiness, induce comfort, promote positive energy, and resonate with our hearts and others. Such objects always create space for so many others such as new experiences, new relationships, new memories, etc while retaining the core of what really and indeed is. The action of parting with our much-liked personal belongings in favor of creating physical space for ourselves is not aimless in terms of emptying out rooms or garages. However, it goes beyond as people have realized that the essence of memories and identity is greater than in the material things that we own; our memories and identity cannot be a mere reflection of our goods as our true lives and our existence are a combination of different things that completely entwine and shape us and are therefore beyond descriptions in time or space.

Embracing Abundance in Simplicity

FOMO is a well-known word. It is the fear of missing out or not being able to be a part of a certain activity or an event that happened. This fear can come from various kinds of things like someone on social media going somewhere interesting or if a few of your friends are planning on going to a great concert and you have not been invited. What we fail to understand is that sometimes we are a part of a certain group of people not having breakfast while those people might look very satisfied and happy. The feeling of missing out is so common because of learning from social media and the friends have been with the change to lead a fulfilled life forget about small talk and it leads them to believe that they do not belong or are inferior to those people. This deep-seated issue makes people uncomfortable and the feeling that they need to be filled these experiences or earn these possessions in an effort to fulfil this void within themselves.

However, the damage that the implementation of FOMO makes to our minds might be deep. The way we feel about everything is often dictated by what we see on the internet and the same cycle still continues, where we believe that buying a new phone from Apple or being a part of an influencers event can fulfil our desires and make everything better. What we fail to understand is that this is only a temporary state of enjoyment that immediately passes when we start focusing on the next big event or a purchase and that on and on, we go without actually living in the moment and appreciating it. Not only does this affect our relationship with the physical because it is easy to accumulate stuff, but it also makes it hard to appreciate everything around us and makes us feel as though we have full lives.

Hence, we can conclude that the time has come to free ourselves from FOMO and embrace the power of freedom choice, being happy with the present, and what we feel. Minimalism is a lifestyle that is probably the starkest antithesis to the connotation of FOMO. It is about living as if you consciously choose to get whatever it is you wish for and to know that what you want is right here. And while the world beyond attempts to sate this yearning for the newest, best and most typically, our memories recognize all emergencies, events and moments in our being. This attempt, when combined with our ability to leave and the right choice of how to best live life in its many colours, is more captivating than 'doing more' as broader as 'having more' in as past as 'being more'.

It is not that bad to put an end to killing yourself and trying to fill with all these things your reality. What is there still to do for people who do not wish to 'miss out'? Choice is ours. We can start changing the way that we consume social media. Comparing our lives with those of the people we want on Instagram as aspirational does not mean we have to be more thankful for what we have now. It means that rather than thinking, "I wish I had that", we should realize that, "I have given up something in my life or I have really enjoyed this experience". Take a note and write only one sentence: what is it that you think you have been missing these days and how will you help fill that hole instead? Social media should also be looked at in terms of connection and engagement. Use the time you spent scrolling to call a friend, visit a neighbor, or hit the gym and you will have meaningful conversations and connect more meaningfully with the people around you.

From ask yourself and serve yourself questions to change the way you think about your life and all that may be going on and do a step closer to living the life you wish. Try to fill each day with at least one new thing and change your perception of them so that they set the tone for the rest of your day. This is how for example you could do it in the Affirmation app by answering eight questions in about eight minutes. The first question would be, "Are you organized?" The answer would be "I am organized", "I am good at organizing things", and "I have a good number of people in my life who can

When we examine FOMO's potential as an impediment to our happiness, we find that minimalism presents us with a viable alternative to its all-consuming grip by stressing the importance of being present. Instead of dwelling on the things we may lack or the things we may miss out on, minimalism challenges us to go within ourselves and search for that which is significant in our lives and helps us make decisions that resonate with our convictions. It's a mode of existence that emphasizes having a few invaluable things that give one meaning and satisfaction, thus allowing a person to realize that having less can offer a far richer and fuller life than chasing after material things that lack depth or meaning. In this state of being, material desire and a frantic chase of more ever-elusive experiences disappear and are replaced by the clear yet tough thought that perhaps all the other things we have been yearning so hard for can actually be replaced by the rich life-experiences and the few carefully chosen possessions that a person holds so dearly.

Gratitude is perhaps the first antidote to FOMO, a preventative measure against discontent that focuses on the present and what we have. It helps us realize the importance of the things we have in our possession, as well as our relationships, jobs, classes, and all other things that we might have taken for granted over time. Whenever we take a moment each day to take stock of the good things in our lives, whether that be loved ones, comfortable living spaces, or daily moments of joy, we create a strong mindset that counters the need to chase after everything desirable that seems to be in the market. When we are grateful, we are able to let go of the artificiality of the media and marketing that point us in the direction of dissatisfaction with what we have. Gratitude thus has the power of shifting our attention where for a long, limiting mentality would have focused on what is lacking. Instead gratitude enables us to see life as it is and to focus our attention on the fact that we are not missing anything crucial but rather have all that is necessary or a lot indeed in many cases.

An additional, very effective way of ameliorating the state of affairs that FOMO creates in us is by re-examining the way we have been defining success and happiness for ourselves. In our modern society, success often is equated with spending money, attaining certain social status, and packing as many experiences into life as possible. Yet at the very heart of minimalism, there is a belief that what is actually maximally important and should define our success and happiness is whether or not we are living in accordance with our own values and leading a simple life enriched by such values. One might make a choice to slow down and stop, and intentionally live a meaningful life with focus on experiencing a very few and dear things. In the same spirit, it may mean ignoring the cult of popularity and prestige that surrounds us and choosing to develop those few close relationships that are actually precious for us rather than those with many followers on Facebook or Instagram. By taking upon ourselves the burden of establishing our definitions of success and happiness, we manage not to be influenced by the demoralizing societal standards that press us into the search of material possessions or the degree of other people's appreciate.

The key to overcoming the fear of missing out, otherwise known as FOMO, is to focus on what truly brings joy and fulfilment into one's life. The act of deliberately taking time to identify the things in life that matter most and give a sense of value and meaning rather than just following in the footsteps of others or giving in to the pressure of society to do this or that. For some people, this could mean taking regular time out from daily routines to spend time with significant others, following a hobby, engaging in a spiritual practice, or partaking in activities for self-care. Others may require identifying and decluttering their environment to create a calm and inspiring environment that supports a conscious way of living. By being conscious of the choices we make and how they relate to our beliefs and wants, we can create lives that are focused on meaning and personal evolution and not on the endless pursuits of activities and possessions.

Mindful consumption, which means being as intentional as possible with what we choose to invite into our lives whether those be material things, experiences, or even commitments, is also vital when it comes to dealing with the feeling of missing out in life. Instead of living in constant anxiety that arises from unfulfilled needs due to the pressure that comes from wanting what others have, we could rather pause and reflect on whether this thing or experience genuinely adds any desirable value into our lives at all. Is it compatible with our purpose and beliefs? Will it develop into a thing that we will cherish for some time or is it only a passing moment? When we focus our awareness on these questions, we realize that we are able to make better decisions regarding our purchases and avoid accumulating unnecessary clutter both physically and in our hearts as a result of snapping up all that is offered by this shopping world.

Another critical step on the path towards the normal condition of freedom from the fear of missing out concerns creating supportive environments consisting only of other people who share similar objectives and values as ourselves. When surrounded by people, who tend to think in quite similar ways or rather espouse philosophies that obey the minimalist statute, it becomes much less likely that one shall be required to succumb to beliefs about possessions or experiences being compulsory parts of a fulfilling existence instead of optional. A group such as this could boost one's encouragement, lend its support, and spur individuals into action thereby enabling them to achieve their personal goals without being distracted by trends among the rest of the society. Additionally, this group creates a sense of community bas. A feeling of being connected with other human beings can help overcome some of the basic fears that underlie the fear of missing out.

Another powerful approach that can actually help people get rid of the fear of missing out is to learn to be mindful of whatever it is that is happening at the time, which is called being present. Much of the time we are caught in the fear of missing out because we are thinking about the future — about the things that we might miss, why the people might be having certain experiences that we can only experience if we would have done something differently. However, we can practice mindfulness and learn to focus our attention elsewhere, in the present, and this can help us deal with some of these worries. Being present enables us to focus on the moment and appreciate the many amazing things that we are currently doing and enjoying and instead of focusing on what might be denied us. It enables us to fully let ourselves into and enjoy the wonder that is right here and now.

In the end, it is crucial to appreciate that FOMO is a part of humanity. It is only human to be drawn towards wanting to know what other people are engaged in or to be left pondering if we are making the right choices in life. Minimalism, on the other hand, teaches us not to let the fear of loss direct us. We can acknowledge it, analyze it, and then choose a path that is authentic to ourselves. By adopting the core values of minimalism as intentionality, simplicity, and focusing on what is really important to us, we can rise above the fear of missing out and create a life that is more than just bloated with events or possessions but rather one that is highly fulfilling and meaningful. Minimalism gives us the power to stop focusing on what other people have and shift our focus to what we really want as a lifestyle option.

When we choose the path of minimalism, we get to a point where we eventually trust that it is not about the things that we are missing that is equally about the things that are truly important in our lives. A life that is truly lived is not about piling up as much acquisition as one can grasp; rather, it is about making conscious choices that have meaning in our lives based on our core principles and to be true to them. Thus, we are able to change from a perspective of lack and feeling unfulfilled in its embrace to that of surplus and intense satisfaction where every decision we make communicates who we are and what we hold dear. It is only when we focus on what really matters and what brings meaning to our lives that we can begin to confront the fear of missing out and to embrace a life without guilt, struggle, and no fear, but a life full of adventure, love, and growth.

Sustaining the Minimalist Path

It can be unbelievably impressive to make the adoption of minimalism because it is something that makes hitherto and impossible endeavours to come to reality, the process of getting rid of things that are no longer needed, making one's living conditions simple, neat, and orderly, and finally not to be concerned with superficial things buy. It is a unique experience where the person's focus is shifted from what is not important to the essence of life and standard human life itself is enhanced. It is clear as the one who believes in minimalism and enters with eagerness to be free of all distracts, and crave a deeper truth on the earth have to get stuck and lose the zeal for minimalism a few years later. People around us open doors again and again, or suggest to us that the more we have to consume, the more it will be worthwhile, or that we will be lacking every so often like advertisements and recommendations that appear on the internet as well as those from society as a whole. To practice living in minimalism consistently and to retain its advantages and well-being, one must complicate his/her journey with purpose, analysis and the search for novel ideas that would keep him/her motivated. In this piece, the author reflects on certain techniques that assist in remaining committed to a minimalist approach to living and how the same can be pursued in a conscious and in-depth manner.

Besides developing a philosophy and life objective, go back to what is essential a few times a year to stay geared up in minimalism and review the knowledge his/her belief system is based on. Minimalism is not a popular entertainment that a person gets into and out of; it is a manner of life that continues depending on one's commitment and decision to act in such a particular way. Ahead, the body transitions one receives, and the assurance of slipping back to the past, causing disturbing tensions, during some tiny times in the course of the way, becomes almost unavoidable. As it is common in the course of life, minimalism as a fundamental component of the individual's life is bound to be uninterruptedly changing with the people in my life altering, with new experiences coming, as well as with my beliefs questioning. To avoid reminiscing and recommitting to minimalism, both on specified occasions and as part of an intentional way of living, one must carry out an examination to see if he/she is at par with the ultimate belief enlargement.

It is in examining straight what are the transcendental values and life goals and in doing what can hamper the complication of our reduced case that we grow again in clarity and purpose. What is it that makes me heart? What are my attitudes to life? How do I wish to utilize my time together with the same things? What elevates my spirit? Therefore, asking such questions helps one clarify the purpose in life therefore helps one strengthen his/her knowledge of what the essence of a simple lifestyle is. It is thus essential to be limited by such a state that is manipulable and adjustable time and time again even to pressure and the feedback of the outside world. With well-defined principles, one is better equipped to fight the incessant bombarding from advertising, social media, and the dictates that surround them as a whole and that society represents. Such situations allow a person to learn how to channel on their actual values and live a life full of a purpose and enjoyment for the brief time that they remain on the earth.

There is another effective way in which one can rely on and stay motivated through the principles of minimalism which is called getting the assumptions regularly by looking at one's acknowledging and even questioning the possessions he/she has together with the habitual activities in life, if there are any. Minimalism is a process that does not involve achieving and settling for a specific, consistent static state of perfection but instead, it is the process of having life simplified and refined continually. With the passage of time, it can be penny-wise to acknowledge that the strategies and principles that were useful to us last year may not still work for us today which means that we should know what really matters in our lives and be prepared to let go and liberate ourselves from those things that no longer help us. This may entail tracking the sources of clutter in the house, going back to the routines we practice daily, and even going as far as thinking about those commitments that we had and now feel as a burden and some form of weight that is held on us.

As one gets to look into and question the possessions and the habitual things in their lives, they also get to develop their knowledge base and enhance their understanding and experience of the minimalism principles. By doing this one effectively prevents the lifestyle from becoming static or repetitious in which there is nothing new as regards minimalism conception. Instead of being docile and having a life that has been mechanized, such reflection guarantees that we stay mindful, engaged, and deliberate in our decision-making. By questioning the belongings that are genuinely essential in life and the things that can be gotten rid of in the process we end up with a living environment and way of life that utilizes such simplicity to fit who we are as individuals and that which we hold dear at any given time. It should therefore be noted that this process of a constant reshaping of the life of one individual is important as far as the idea of minimalist living being taken to the long run is concerned.

Another way in which the motivation can be achieved while living a minimalistic life is through the idea of engaging oneself in new minimalist challenges that keep on sprucing things up. These challenges can come in various forms; they may include a month-long no-buy period within which one cannot buy any new goods, a digital detox in which the person tries to do without any digital gadget, or a capsule wardrobe that helps save space.

These Arctic openings and challenges drive us beyond the status quo and help us to discover new and interesting ways through which minimalistic ideas can be practiced in our signature style and also live intentionally. What's more, the way this acts on the minimalist road is to create and bring into it a new lease of life in the sense that the road does not stagnate or becomes boring but rather, it is continuously exciting and full of life. When we engage in new challenges while at the same time completing them, we slowly keep in check our drive to a life of minimalism, discover new things that the principles have to offer to our lives, and weave such circumstances into the fabric of our lives.

For individuals who feel overwhelmed with environmental distractions and the vast array of life choices, there is a dire need to be inspired more than once a day. Finding additional motivation through communities, books, or documentaries centered around minimalism is one invaluable means through which minimalist practices may be kept alive in one's life. Minimalism is not just about changing one's exterior but also changing their way of looking at things and connecting with people who surround them with the same feelings as they do. Whenever we occur to be concerned via this community, scored through these series online or even in real life, we can come up with the sense of being completed while fighting through and sticking to the system of minimalism. In this community of people, you can learn from them, share your experiences, and see how others have overcome tough situations when trying to live a simple yet meaningful life. It's that knowledge of knowing you're not alone and being with others who are also pursuing the same ideals that create this connection and support that most us possibly need during times of trouble in when traveling with minimum possessions. And there is nothing better than being surrounded by likeminded people who share the same vision in life or at least have goals to be happy and full in such a way.

The internet is filled with a lot of good documentaries and articles that have been able to change the lives of many individuals and also inform them about minimalism. There are many resources out there such as books and documentaries which can inspire and also motivate those who are trying to transition into a simpler lifestyle. Minimalism is one lifestyle and it can be practical and inspiring. By consuming written or audio-visual content about the lives of other minimalists or watching documentaries about the need for living a simpler life, it would be hard not to be motivated by their ways of life. Most of the time it's easy to slip back due to negativity and lack of confidence, but these experiences will definitely bring you back to positive feelings and reasoning as to why you got interested in minimalist lifestyle in the first place. Minimalism is about making personal choices as to how we want to shape our surroundings. Through books, we learn about the adaptation of minimalism and the time that is spent on these lives. Through documentaries, we amp ourselves with energy from the visual impact of minimalism and lifestyle change. Making small changes is difficult if you feel isolated and disheartened by others' experiences and stories, but if you continually feel changed such a way that fitting in with other people's experiences, it becomes so much easier to take those first step(s) on the path towards becoming a minimalist.

The next important pillar of motivation in the context of minimalism is acknowledging the good things that this approach brings into our lives. There is a tendency of the people to concentrate on what we do not have, what we had to lose, and how much more we had to relinquish whenever it comes to minimalism. But when this happens, the focus shifts away from the positive aspects that are inherent in the minimalistic living. To begin with, the optimal attitude should be adopted while scrutinizing minutely the positive changes that the implementation of minimalism in our lives has had like the decline in stresses, the increased freedoms, or the clearer thoughts. This is the way we tolerate the destruction and fall into a kind of depression when we assume the negative approach when taking part in minimalism since that being said, we all chose to get this change. Rather, it is important to concentrate on the gifts that minimalism brings into our lives and the ways it can help us grow and develop toward happier and successful human beings. Anything can be taken as stressful in today's world, especially when we have to take more than we can consume. However, upon reflection, it may

Looking at motivation within minimalism reminds us that motivation is not necessarily a constant state but can fluctuate similar to the tides. The journey of minimalism has a certain excitement and fun factor tied to it that unfortunately will sometimes wane or fade away even as we are doing it. There may be days when working with minimalism is more difficult than usual due to other priorities in life. At such times we must practice kindness towards ourselves and recognize the fact that minimalism is not a race that must be completed but rather a way of life that will have both paid explanation and involvements in it. It would be appropriate, yes even expected, to have some moments of reflection time out for re assessment of our goals in minimalism and then returning prepared to work on them as per our readiness when we feel right. The main thing about this process is not the little, everyday challenges but rather the objectives that are evolving at this moment concerning what minimalism really means to you and the purposes of the choices that we are making out of the practice.

Moreover, maintaining optimism about minimalism is continually choosing to apply the viewpoint of abundance stemming from simplicity, as opposed to seeing it as poverty or limiting. It is a tendency to view minimalism imposed on oneself as some form of gift deprivation; however, these restrictions on material wealth enable an abundance last longer and deeper in many areas of existence: the gift of time, the gift of freedom, and opportunities for creativeness, and especially human interactions. That is precisely in the course of minimizing the superfluity and letting go of the unnecessary we find and prioritize those things that are dear to us; it makes freedom from the limits of our minds possible, entering into a world we did not know existed before. When we see the present frame of mind it is transferring our perception that minimalism is not restricting oneself to access what is harmful or not needed but availing us with choices and capacities that could bring us to experience life much more abundantly and meaningfully. By taking a grip of this rich philosophy not only do we stay inspired by It but also position ourselves positively in the application of this notion.

To conclude, following a minimalistic way of life primarily means trust by identifying what we want and those insights that help us lead a simplistic and deliberate life. It worries about being updated and not repeating life as we know it but instead makes conscious decisions about what to include in our lives and reflects on what we value and find interesting or lacking. Acknowledging the notion of minimalism and purging it becomes an emotionally recharged undertaking whereby our simplifying practices and attitudes will not only make us lead happy lives but also make us genuinely happy despite less in our homes and the fact that we pay more attention to what matters. On a regular basis returning to your universal values with what matters the most, doing new things, looking for popular stuff out there, and celebrating the positive things about minimalism allows us to keep it alive and moving; to be able to adjust this way of living and thus be able to use it in every moment of our present days, still drawing from its simple beauty and valuable riches. With the right mindset, perspective, and practices in place, minimalism can be an authentic lifestyle that resonates deeply with ourselves today, generates satisfaction and significance on our journey of life as well as the lives of those close to us tomorrow.

Harmonising Minimalism in Relationships

Embarking on the journey of minimalism can undoubtedly feel like a quest of epic proportions that is as personal as the journey can be while still providing certain life benefits for family and friends. Nevertheless, if minimalism is attempted to be applied to groups like families and friends, certain difficulties come into view as an unfortunate consequence of the one-size-fits-all style of minimalism. Disparities between family members, partners, or colleagues with different approaches to ownership, consumption of goods, and fat conditions can lead to tension or disputes. It nearly always takes a lot of understanding, conversation, and a steady willingness to compromise to try and change the way that people live, consume, and work in one's environment. The end goal in such matters should not be to arm-twist others into accepting one's minimalist values but rather to focus on creating an environment where the needs of all parties concerned are taken care of and their aspirations do not infringe upon those of other members of the group.

One of the most common causes of hatred in relationships where minimalism can be a factor is varying views of the different 'things'. The merely existing, rooms with fewer items and more decorative art do not look uncluttered; one or two lovely mugs are not enough to make a coffee without seeming a lot, rather, the question might be a little more complicated. On the other hand, some people are at peace with the existence of more items or merely want to possess more items in their surroundings to feel complete about their life. The differences in this regard can sometimes have their roots in our childhoods, customs, and experiences in life. For instance, a person who grew up in a society where material affluence was the order of the day may be more left out of the bondedness with thing as a way of holding onto wealth because this is what they grew up knowing while those who were fortunate enough to have come from wealthy backgrounds may not be so emotionally involved with objects.

When these conflicting attitudes about belongings present themselves in a relationship, it is of utmost importance to first approach the matter with a calm demeanor and understanding. Instead of thinking of the other person as a packrat, and telling the other person that their feelings do not matter at the moment, take time to listen more carefully and understand the other person's remarks regarding the significance that certain items or practices hold for them. By affirming the points of view of the other party and recognizing their worries to a certain degree, one actually lays the basis for a dialogue of mutual admiration and respect, where the comments made by both sides are received without any form of evaluation.

Effective communication is one of the most important abilities that a person should possess if he or she wants to confront the many cultural differences that are likely to arise in the society. In particular, when trying to introduce minimalism to a spouse, relative or roommate, it is vital to present the topic of minimalism in a positive way that will not Tend to draw negative criticisms or judgment to the other party which could in turn lead to resistance. For instance, when using more accusatory phrases such as just saying, "You have too much stuff" or "We need to get rid of all this clutter," it would be more effective to talk about one's own experience with minimalism and how it has changed his or her life. Thus, if one was to say, "I have noticed that since I started out with minimalism, my personal stress levels have decreased and my focus has increased significantly. I feel like this experience is quite fundamental and would love for you to experience the same." When you stick to the favorable perspectives and experiences that have occurred in your life without appearing to criticize what another person has or deny them any existence in their life, you are most likely to receive a valid response. As a result, a more positive and productive dialogue is likely to be developed.

Trying to find common ground where both parties mutually agree on is yet another crucial approach to deal with family and relationship issues that may be caused by minimalism. This approach requires the active identification of those issue areas which draw both parties to agree and building from such a stand without majoring on issues that create disagreements. For instance, despite having different opinions as to what constitutes the essential things and what constitutes trash, one may both agree that having a clutter-free living room can be beneficial for both of them. When one starts from the point of shared values, it becomes easy to try and work towards the same aims rather than to attempt and prove the other party wrong. Hence, it is possible to connect with one's partner and create a team of two who will focus on making their living space a better place for both through effective communication.

To properly embrace a minimalist way of life in a shared space, compromise is yet another essential element. Minimalism is not a binary concept whereby one has to either totally accept it or avoid it altogether; instead, it is about being able to find a middle ground that considers all citizens' wants and inclinations. As an instance, if one partner is more inclined to have minimal ornaments that are particular to a house but the other one prefers to boost the space with more decorative pieces, it is reasonable to agree that public areas of the house like the living room should be minimized while still permitting personal expression in view of the private spaces such as bedrooms or studies. Such a method can create a scenario whereby both parties feel like they have their share of the house and can personalize their spaces according to their needs and wants but at the same time keeping a clean and tidy living space that both can be happy in. As a result, both people are able to enjoy the benefits of minimalism without either feeling like they have to compromise their beliefs or abandon their preferences. In conclusion, minimalism, because of its emphasis on openness, sympathy, and compromise, is a lifestyle that has the potential to make the world a better place.

Leading by example is an impactful and strong method in inspiring family or shared living places to become minimalist. Instead of trying to persuade people around you to practice minimalism, show them how wonderful it is to use minimalism in your life. Other people may be inspired to try minimalism when they see how that has benefited you. These benefits are such as decreased stress, improved focus, and attraction to a simple way of life. Children are especially influenced by the example of their parent's actions and attitudes. If you show them how nice and easy a simple life can be, you will be planting a seed of minimalism as they grow.

But it is also true that minimalism may manifest itself in various ways among people that live together. Some may embrace minimalism at large while some may want just a little bit of it without entirely embracing the new way of living. This is important to respect various modes of doing things as minimalism is not a kind of standard doctrine that can be adopted fully. What matters is for every individual to identify their true color based on this practice and lead a life that feels reasonable and fulfilling. By giving regard for individual preferences and ways of presenting themselves, it is possible to build a more cohesive and encouraging environment supporting all kinds of personalities comfortably.

Living the minimal life through family and relationship dynamics also includes being aware of the different personal perspectives with regard to culture and generations. In certain cultures, a physical possession is closely associated with the organization of the family, the identity of the family, heritage, or social status and having the thought of giving up some of the items can meet a lot of resistance. Similarly, the older people in society who have lived in times where scarcity is a common issue would relate to physical possessions differently from the younger generations that have been brought up in a culture that lays emphasis on consumerism. It is very important for families to realize these discrepancies and accept how their lives have been shaped in as far as minimalism is concerned. Creating an atmosphere where everyone feels it's safe & valued through cultural awareness, acceptance & respect helps families adopt a minimalist lifestyle that is positive and respectful and that enables each individual to progress on their own in a way that feels true to themselves.

Sometimes, it may be helpful to get outside help or resources to cope with these huge dynamics. Books, articles or workshops targeting the subject of minimalism could result in offering great insights and creative strategies for dealing with various challenges. Besides, participating in a minimalist community, whether offline or online, could offer consolation, direction, and the fact that you belong to a group of people who are going through a similar journey. Such resources could be helpful in reinforcing the minimalist mindset and providing practical tools for overcoming difficulties during most family or other forms of communal living.

Ultimately, when it comes to the practice of minimalism in family and interpersonal relationships, it is not about enforcing strict rules or attaining culturally perceived meanings of simple life. It is all about creating a supportive environment suitable for the well-being, happiness, and personal growth of every person involved in the practice. When you approach minimalism with care, respect, and a collaborative spirit, you learn to navigate the Losses & Gains that come with living a more mindful, intentional, and real life, and to enjoy the way to do it, perfectly optimizing it despite the occasional storms of life.

In the process of recognizing minimalism in the context of relationships, we see that simplicity is not only the act of reducing our things but also the act of adding and enriching our connection with one another. Rather, it is the ability to optimize our lives in such a manner that the spiritual, emotional, and physical needs of each individual are met, a system of respect and understanding within the family. Through conscious and considerate conversations, compromises, and actual portrayals that give everyone a first-hand experience of minimalism, it is possible to affect minimalism positively in family relationships in a way that strengthens the family unit and also make each of its members feel fulfilled.

Chapter 9

The Long-Term Impact of Minimalism

Minimalism is often embraced as a response to the overwhelming demands of modern life—an antidote to the clutter, excess, and constant pursuit of more that characterises contemporary society. For many, the initial appeal of minimalism lies in its promise of immediate relief: the clear space, the simplicity, the sense of control regained over one's environment. However, as one continues down the minimalist path, it becomes clear that minimalism is not just a temporary fix or a one-time purge; it is a profound shift in mindset that, when sustained, can have lasting effects on all aspects of life.

The long-term impact of minimalism extends far beyond the physical realm of decluttering and simplifying. It touches the very core of how we live, influencing our decisions, our relationships, and our overall sense of well-being. Minimalism challenges us to continuously align our lives with our most deeply held values and to pursue what truly matters with clarity and intention. It asks us to reconsider our definitions of success, happiness, and fulfillment, and to measure our lives not by what we accumulate but by the richness of our experiences and the authenticity of our choices.

Yet, maintaining the minimalist lifestyle over the long haul is not without its challenges. The initial excitement of clearing out closets and simplifying routines can give way to the more nuanced work of sustaining these changes amidst the pressures and complexities of everyday life. As time goes on, the allure of consumer culture and the demands of modern living can begin to creep back in, making it easy to fall back into old habits. This chapter explores the strategies for sustaining simplicity over the long term, ensuring that minimalism remains not just a passing phase but a permanent and enriching aspect of life.

Living with intentionality is at the heart of this sustained practice. Minimalism is not just about having fewer things; it's about living with purpose, where every decision, from how we spend our time to how we interact with others, is made with mindfulness and deliberation. This chapter delves into the ways in which minimalism encourages us to continually assess and realign our lives with our core values, helping us to navigate life's challenges with a sense of purpose and direction.

As we explore the long-term impact of minimalism, we also reflect on how this lifestyle contributes to enduring happiness and fulfillment. Minimalism offers a path to a deeper kind of contentment, one that is not dependent on external circumstances but is rooted in the simplicity of living true to oneself. By shifting the focus from material possessions and societal expectations to personal well-being and intentional living, minimalism fosters a sense of peace and satisfaction that can sustain us through life's ups and downs.

Finally, this chapter looks ahead to the future of minimalism, considering how this movement might evolve in response to the changing needs and challenges of the world. As minimalism continues to gain traction globally, it holds the potential to shape not only individual lives but also broader societal trends, influencing everything from environmental sustainability to economic practices. The future of minimalism may well be tied to its ability to adapt and remain relevant in a rapidly changing world, offering a vision of a life lived with less but enriched with more meaning, connection, and purpose.

Sustaining Simplicity

Minimizing the number of items in the house that you barely use, therefore mana possess you to at a certain point of view of how you should manage things. We often tend to have minimalism lead to liberation. s being one of the main reasons why people are so fond of it. This is the beauty of minimalism, it positions us on the liberating side. Clinging just to the aspects you cherish is the real game. Furthermore, living out of the rubbish of yesteryear instead of everyday herding of wastes, people prefer to be more close to nature, to look for their peace and value their own existence. The relationship between minimalism and happiness is not about the amount of material but about the brevity and clarity of the presence of things in the living environment. Far from this, minimalism, understood freedom from owning which doesn't have to be addressed through the removal of the material plethora, can curtail intellectual clutter. But now the consumer development in every corner of the world, made children, the future of humanity, the human will soon to lose the minimalism ability and will give the channels of information and update the manner in only the client can understand. It is important to mention how minimalism can teach both children and students what can be formulated from nothing and what is thought to be necessary to have to make life complete. However, similar to the case with sports and diets, adopting minimalistic lifestyle does not exempt the followers from the challenges that usually come along with such a significant change. The latent excitement along the practicing of minimalism can lose its sparkle with times. Thus, the simplicity and depth it bringing by minimalism are being constrained only by the way of thinking and willingness of people.

Enlarging the telemetry of going forward with minimalism to the sustenance of it without mixing unnecessary issues with it is necessary to promote minimalism. Persons who rush to obtain newer minimalist tools in their bid for a simpler life often overlook the sustainability of the new acquisitions. Until the strong influx of the bus back into the old commercial hub, people need intent of the willful buying of necessary items instead of just following their minds and getting different impractical things. Not until green energy developers change community ideas towards environment and clean energy, and train people to do the same, problematic wealth distribution will be tackled and rural people's standard of living improved. One of the underlying reasons behind the difficulty encountered by the learners is that it requires authentic participation, that is, one has to be in a real learning context. However; we still have to bear in mind the role of education in the future for its potential design and creativity which are the key traits for highly skilled employment in the future. Additionally, electric vehicles are too expensive, and not all consumers will race to acquire one or more as an alternative to their gasoline automobiles. This undertaking is, I think, not simple nor safe, but for the most part, it is ideal and sound.

Regardless of how open we may be or how hard we may try, the environmental crisis may bring us an unforgivable result, earth's destruction, the loss of our resources, and finally, even our freedom as society has already been several years under the rule of green policies, etc. Each of us is responsible for refusing, reducing, and recycling the disposal of plastic in our environment and at work to minimize the effects of global warming. Such utilization or alternatives can solve multiple problems already facing the planet by humans, and finding a new source of energy is much better than the exploitation of animals. Although these points are valid, we cannot ignore the fact that human activities are the leading cause of ozone layer depletion; deforestation being the greatest. One trend which seems to be developing in cultural studies is the many of the societal changes which were formerly prescribed by others have now been assumed by the people themselves.

The inclusion of some of the questions such as the ones given above will bring a different level of students' thinking about the issues related to SIO.

A statement to the effect that the church in Zimbabwe was increasingly involved in political and economic activity)` would have been a more appropriate opening to the discussion. Moreover, countries in the third world need to respond to the challenge of the aging population by redesigning, restructuring, and reorienting their policies and institutions.() A rise in the number of road construction sites causing burdens to the environment and people due to noise, dust, and over-use of facilities (e.g. water) must be considered and solutions should be quickly devised now that the technology is well advanced and cheaper. This is how, the layers of sand in the desert would have entirely disappeared, and their aeroplane would have probably sunk in the sand. Change is a process that takes place over time and there is no way to predict or achieve the final result immediately; the state of nature is a continuous process without a reason. This paper will examine how the advances in technology have contributed to the growth and globalization of the auto industry and how the impacts of technology on the socio-economic environment have changed the lives of people?

Global warming has always been an aspect of concern due to the severe impact on the environmental conditions and human health since fast fashion was invented along with many other environmental problems such as pollution, acid rain, the depletion of the ozone layer, and the waste of natural resources. After being produced, and then sold, and eventually disposed of, fashion on the other hand, takes priority over environmental concern. For some, profit is more important than the environmental impact, as they argue that there are alternatives in case of declining resources. The apparel industries, especially the manufacturing ones, have been organized upon characteristics of a leaner (smaller) workforce which ensures adaptability and modernization of production. Moreover, I feel that the current keeper of earth's reign in the celestial spheres (through the gravitational sensation) is not giving rest to the great planet but is causing stress to the whole universe.

Nevertheless, recycling materials saves energy and produces lesser greenhouse gas emissions, and many are turning to this alternative. Furthermore, their usage has been advocated as a potential solution to climate change with many promoting them as a carbon-neutral alternative. A more careful reading into the future stock market trends shows that companies that sustain their economic benefits alongside ecological concerns will be ahead while those who persist in making unwise environmental decisions will be left behind. Sure, a lot can be done if all the countries exchanging the greenhouse emissions could faithfully and dutifully carry on the respective programs as indicated but the necessity is to monitor the performance of developed and developing states concerning their pledges on the reduction of gas emissions. This could be because the cities are overpopulated, and the administration is incapable of providing basic amenities like sanitation, healthcare, and education to the citizens. As previously stated, the unauthorized copying of software is a copyright infringement and constitutes an offense under the Copyright Act. Hence, if actually there are any software issues, such as viruses, they might be affecting your websites in some way.

Food insecurity is to some extent worsened by the inadequacy of long-term investment in food production and supply areas `and national agricultural and rural development. However, unlike the big-market groceries, the independent consumer has the ability to choose to purchase genocide-free products and avoid corrupt dealings in the business world. The "infrastructure" has always been one of the most fundamental levers for the sustainable development of societies while the "superstructure" has been the main deterrent force inhibiting that progress.

Your priority to minimalism must be at least in one situation where you would rather choose habits (that are minimalistic) instead of always buying them from a store as our society consists of people from the upper levels of the market. Because every single thing is all about case by case, foreign countries have the right to either stop or limit whatever they want. Take the example of Taiwan, Taiwan has been a part of Hong Kong for a very long period. Despite the fact that, all developed countries as like for example India, which is one of the biggest pollution sectors can produce their pollution-free power. In short, the process of language acquisition is a multifaceted and multi-domain process which involves various skills being gestated and channeled in a learner through a bridge of motivation and reinforcement.

Learning is not a one-time happening but rather a project of ongoing assessments that requires appropriate time provisions and involvement of all learners. According to the narrator, the asylum would never have been discovered if Holmes had not been there. God's message was conveyed loud and clear to everyone and in a loving way. If we look at the last 100 years we can see that the society has changed both culturally and socially as well as in technology. That had a huge impact on the female rights movement empowered by the tech-driven opportunity for jobs and more security instead of forcing them to rely on the physical labor of a husband. Among dynamic perspectives which include language and culture, technological advances have created teaching stories which will result in long-term improvement if involved properly.

Even as the question is serious and challenging, it is absolutely a question of real existence and one that could very well be asked. A team of ten and more colleagues from different places of Armenia, who have a plastic collection initiative, can place suggestions about the need of reusing plastic for the purpose of establishing the water recirculation. The Vietnamese military also possesses a rapid and advanced infrastructure and is the potential producer of complex weapons such as fighter planes and other modern army equipment. Industry efficiency can be enhanced by the upliftment of the structure, more controllable human data interfacing with the computer."

The utilization of gadgets, if directed to enhance environmental studies, especially wildlife research, should be given more encouragement. The digital teaching and learning methods are needed to make changes in content as well as the rules and teaching traditions established since the start. Learning can only take place when the student becomes conscious of language acquisition and is motivated enough to engage in its learning activity. Doing "human watch" is another way to stop destruction even if we cannot change stuff we do not like. However, it was not completed and interrupted due to non-avoidable factors such as breakdown, not complying with the task requirements, and file corruption. The data are in the view that at these high seasons of tourism and recreation and when the temperature of the sea is favorable, human beings are more likely to get close to such aquatic environments which the tortoises inhabit and, therefore, provoking the animals, thereby forming one of the most negative trends in the ecosystem.

Living with Intentionality

Living with intentionality is a serious philosophical measure that combines harmoniously with the smallest ideas of minimalism. This way of life requires at least will to be always in alignment with desired values, thoughts, and the environment. To live an intentional life is also an act of mindfulness, not just a matter of jumping from one task to another without a second thought. On the contrary, an individual who practices modulated thinking first re-orientates their lives to gain a clear vision of where they are heading and then making decisions that can accomplish their desired way of living.

The way towards intentional living is mostly aided by the minimalist's skill of tidying up physical spaces. Although, this is a tiny portion of the process. Nevertheless, the wider range of ridding that living worth less alive. Not only to one's material possessions, but also to their commitments, relationships, and ways they function. This procedure of filtration allows the individual to concentrate on the main ingredients of his life. Then the mind is at ease to accept what frees its soul the most.

While progressing on the way of intentional living, a thing that becomes an absolute necessity is self-reflection. Introspective practice is a compass that directs people back to their core values when different situations in life become a danger to their lives. This is often a daily period when alone time is allocated regularly to quiet reflection, say, through meditation or some mindful breathing exercises. The moments of tranquillity, on the other hand, give an opportune break to express oneself in such a way that the realization of one's short term goals becomes an integral part of it.

Besides, journaling is revaled as a mighty weapon in the hand of one who seizes the moment for himself. It is an act that in itself shows tangible investigation of one's thoughts and feelings because it is for internalizing and therefore, it has a great impact of which one can be aware. Through consistent journaling, orientations and contradictions in actions become visible, so in the end such can be identified and gotten rid of. Also, writing down goals and visioning them takes them out of the ether, gives others a handle on them, and turns them into a goal that induces one to act towards them.

Goal-setting, when approached with intentionality, becomes a nuanced and dynamic process. Rather than just present a list of what one would like the process of creating a goal to be, intentional goal-setting is that which is the result of deep thought about the value of each objective in relation to the large picture one has for his/her life and overall satisfaction. This task includes as well the therapy to ask not what, but why one is planning to accomplish it. This is where examination often follows the dropping of social goals which are not part of the personally driven actions.

The practice of living one's life with intention is far beyond the dimension of self-development. It is intricated into every part of one's life and influences time allocation, how energy is spent, and relationships are built. Thus, in a world that mostly praises business and value creativity, living with intention means to be careful and cautious about partnerships because of the intimate relationship between a person and the whole of his life.

Living the model of time intentionality entitles one a careful choice of the personal schedule as the most important process of its manifestation. This might be achieved by not choosing activities that do not stick so much with the injunctions of one's core values or achievements at the expense of them even if they look favorable. Moreover, it can be manifest as being wholehearted in any moment and concentrating whatever task or person one is into without falling for the insult of the day which is multitasking.

Energy management as such becomes an intentional practice also under the philosophy of intentional living. Gaining an awareness that personal energy is a limited resource prompts individuals to learn to allot it wisely. This might take the shape of setting protective boundaries against things that hurt one's mental and emotional well-being on the one hand or participation in activities that recharge the battery of the individual on the other. The intentional way of handling energy often results in more sustainable and more joyful life, as people acting on their own nature and showing respect to their possible limitations.

Most importantly, intentional living changes greatly the way people approach relationships. Intentional living is moving away from superficial connections to a greater level of bonding which is deeper and more meaningful. This may entail consciously cutting one's social circles down to focus only on a smaller number of high-quality relationships. It also results in greater intentionality in the process, where one actively listens and fully appears for his relatives, instead of just moving through life´s moments with robotic politeness.

A wish to become intentional in life represents a move from one reality to another. It demands a high level of self-awareness and discipline which can be hard to preserve in the middle of life´s constant diversions and requirements. On the other side, it might mean making some unconventional choices that may lead to the refusal or lack of support from others. Due to this, you may feel isolated or misunderstood.

Nonetheless, for such dedicated people, the gains are immeasurable. Living with intentionality brings about an authentic sense of self and a higher purpose of life. It allows the individuals to be their true selves by understanding and creating the life they wish for not the one that is being dictated by the values which are unconsious. This relationship between valuing and doing is characterized by happiness and fulfilment that goes over the shallow joys that come from consumption of goods and recognition from others.

The end-goal of intentional living is the reclamation of a person´s rights over his own life. The awareness that we are not in control of all life´s situations, however, allows us to influence the way we react to them. By practicing mindfulness and purpose in our decision-making, us avoiding any gap we can create our lives that are cared for in a personally fashioned lifestyle. This is minimalism's true life– not just throwing away the unimportant but deliberate decision on a well-lived life.

The Essence of Joy

Less is more, and minimalism is the quantum leap in the process to attain joy. Minimalism in itself is a concept that encourages human beings to look beyond the external success that is superficial and begin the journey on a more intrinsic level of happiness. The journey these people embark on the road toward simplifying their lives brings with it the awareness that there is a complex relationship between material things and their lives. They are themselves happy being with the others and then using the rest of the space for their activities, rather than having everything crowded and suffocated.

Minimalist happiness is not a masochistic act of deprivation but a deliberate choice to live in such a way that it creates the least distress possible, even if it is the hardest thing to do. It teaches individuals to critically analyze the pursuit of success-through the accumulations of goods according to societal norms-and the associated activities that promulgate such socialization. A shift of thinking from material possessions to the profound meaning of life can promote a new age of well-being in personal lives that also spread into other parts of the society.

One of the most impactful aspects of minimalism is the liberty to break free from the bonds imposed by society to keep up with its expectations externally. We are free from excessive belongings and commitments when we let go of those we do not really need, and develop space for self-actualization and self-discovery. Through the process of recovery from gadget addiction, the truth becomes apparent. The joy arising from the better communication, the peace of the mind due to the clean house, or the happiness of pursuing, for example, a project far exceeds pleasure of just taking a time good.

At the same time, leading a lifetime of minimalism happiness, which is a little different from traditional methods of assessing happiness, is rather a complex endeavor. The conventional standards of living- success in economics, the magnificence of the properties can hardly catch the essence of such a lifestyle. Therefore, we should find ways that show the quality of our internal environment. A manufacturer can provide tools such as self-assessment sheets to be used as a means to the same end of grading work and keeping track of personal development. These may include, for one, releasing periodical literature in which a group member expresses a moment of contentment, a sense of purpose, and overall life satisfaction.

Additionally, observing a reduction in stress can be employed as [an] alternative effective technique to measure the benefits of minimalism. It is commonly found that the process of decluttering living standards significantly aids people to cope better with anxiety and other mental health concerns. It is pertinent to consider a number of procedures such as charting sleep quality, monitoring cortisol levels, or noting incidences of symptoms like: headaches, irritability, and anxiety if one wants to be absolutely sure of the conversion. The fresh mental clarity that accompanies the minimalist way of life can lead to better judgment and more power in controlling one's life.

Mental recovery becomes the most significant resource that minimalism grant. One interesting initial finding that has been produced is that the path of the people living this life is not only maintained but they also develop a new sense of awareness. The way a person spends the freed-up time and whether they have more time now to do the important things in life can be indicators of the positive effects of the lifestyle. Are you now more open to hobbies you had put aside for a long time? Are you now spending more quality time with loved ones? These reallocations can directly influence one's sense of well-being.

'Eudaimonia' is one of the concepts which are often understood as human flourishing or prosperity, its application can provide helpful insight into how minimalism can influence the type of happiness felt- it differs significantly from simple pleasure. Happiness based on pleasure and the avoidance of pain is considered hedonic happiness whereas eudaimonic wellbeing is the real feeling of contentment which arises from living a virtuous life and fulfilling one's potential. The concept of minimalism is almost identical to this in that it draws people's attention to their self-growth, their relationship to others, and the contribution to problems bigger than themselves.

Those who have embraced minimalism as a way of living get to experience and see the world from a different perspective. The constant pursuit of consumerism has been increasingly replaced by understanding the already present and a lack of too much of anything. This appreciation is one of the strongest sources of happiness, as it is independent of external situations or acquisitions. The first skill that can sustain such a person through the many facets of life is the art of having joy despite something difficult.

One must realize that the journey to minimalism and the accompanying happiness may well be the most unique for each person. What fills one with joy and happiness is different for each of us. Therefore, any attempt to come up with a scale to measure happiness here should be far from generalized. People must frequently ponder their lives, with a view to a possibility of continual appraisal and reformulation of these plans in order for them to fit the standards of lived truth and mastery.

The minimalistic effect does not spare other people relations, those at work, and the community in general. When people opt for and are more conscious of their choices and more present in relationships, they are likely to get better at interpersonal relations. The impact of the ripple effect in terms of the connection of the broader community and its consequent relationship satisfaction needs to be mentioned as well.

Success at minimalism, primarily, is the capacity to function on a comfortable level with no overwhelming factors but the items and ideas which closely comply with the individual's values and motives. It is a construction of a life where the outer world reflects the inner values of the person where they are free to do whatever they want and enjoy themselves without the burden of the rest of this world. This parallels the human psyche by creating an experience that is both joyful and profoundly enduring.

As life goes on, difficulties continue, and life continues to be tricky with the nonstop message- the more, the better, minimalism has brought about a breath of fresh air. It is a stark reminder that happiness and fulfillment are not in the heap of goodies but in the beauty of life, the growth of relationships, and the congruence of our actions with our highest principles. The rule of psychological happiness and the absence of pain that is activated by factors in a person is not the case with the sense of well-being; it is based on the right-to-existence ethical value system and the fulfillment of the highest potential.

Minimalism Tomorrow

The phrase "New minimalism" or "The future of minimalism arms humankind with lots of opportunities to the world that is quickly changing" can be a reason to rejoice people because a constant question nowadays is about the development of global technology through taking the minimalistic approach of using less and conserving resources in general. We are going through the most daunting international challenges not only to save the planet but to stick to the principles of minimalism that basically invite rethinking human consumption, happiness, and ownership. This idea, having its roots in sustainability and anti-consumerism, could also achieve positive adjustment and new paths of development with respect to environmental issues.

In the list of issues where minimalism should be the focal point of action, environmental sustainability is in the first place. The more the natural resources are running out and the more the atmosphere is being polluted, the more the ascetic approach of 'less is more' would not be a personal option but the way of life for everybody. Many predicted scenarios may precisely transpire, therefore, an increase in the investment of more durable goods in the form of circular economy can help make way for a better society. The changes in human perception can even reflect on the urban scale. Places could change to being a shared community affair and thus, make recycling and minimizing waste an innovative way to strengthen connections within communities.

Minimalist principles are likely to bring innovation to the urban planning too, the present situation in the future might alter significantly. If the future cities tend to have the small space but multifunctional houses that are not only efficient but also very pleasant to live in, the city landscape is going to be different. Public spaces may be planned to facilitate engagement and shared encounters, as opposed to private enjoyment. Small environment-friendly homes that are specifically designed for essential needs, yet are also space-age tech marvels, could be the hottest selling item of the coming period.

Schools can also be among the systems advancing the minimalist approach, focusing on basic skills and knowledge instead of overwhelming students with information. This could lead to a cleaner, more customised approach to knowledge that puts critical thinking, creativity, and adaptability on the line instead of just routine memorization. Schools might offer students a lot of opportunities to learn by experimenting and receiving instructions on how to do things, which are of utmost importance in a world where quick fix and resourcefulness are highly valued.

However, technology, something that at first sight seems contradictory to minimalism, could in fact, become minimalisms' greatest comrade. As machines become more and more powerful, and the world is run by automation, there are predictions that technologies of the future will be so small that we won't even see them. The idea of living without the disruption of technology is already a possibility and can be proved through such concepts as digital minimalism. This idea recommends making use of computers without getting into overusing them.

The abstract 'minimalism' could also have a role in the solution of the economic inequality problem. For instance, minimalism; by contradicting the popular belief that joy comes from material things, can be the factor, the starting point in the reassessment of the economic systems. The chances of seeing public policy or private business assert the quality of life metrics over pure economic growth, in other words, the kind of policies prioritizing well-being, leisure time, and accessibility of services more than the gathering of wealth and consumption is also on the horizon.

The realization of the pragmatic approaches of minimalism is not without challenges, however. One major obstacle could be the attempt of corporate culture to convert the minimalist aesthetics into mere products of consumer culture. We've witnessed 'minimalist products' being marketed as luxury goods, sectionally tearing apart the original idea of minimalist. Furthermore, the movement should intensify its resistance to such merchandising by underlining that the original minimalism is not about tangible, visual aesthetics but it's at the heart of mindset and values.

Moreover, the rapid change of technology and social standards is one of the challenges. As new technological advances are developing and social norms are shifting, upholding the minimalist values may demand recurrent reevaluations and adaptiveness. The campaign for simplicity is going to find real difficulties in maintaining its core values while providing enough elasticity for dealing with new problems as well as new opportunities.

To keep its relevance and also to stay powerful, minimalism will need to change its focus from individual lifestyle choices. The next phases of development might prioritize the contributions from the group as well as the mental turn for the governments knowing that handling the real decrease lies within the society. This might be through proposing legislative changes, launching projects that implement environment-friendly business values, and raising public awareness about minimalist living to create a sustainable and attractive future for everybody.

Minimalism in the future can be progressing towards a more diverse and inclusive society where people of different cultures can find a common ground, and still exist in their unique ways. This is the center of most exigencies addressed above and the concept of minimalism as a single point of the simplest and simplest way to have the same idea render different notion of intercultural practices to people. In a broader sense social diffusions occur so it needs that relevant cultural elements embrace diversity which will be a result of localized and simplified sequences. There will be many forms of minimalism, each arising from local traditions but united by the same principles, each adding to the already existing diversity of the world.

Ultimately, the future of minimalism is highly dependent on its capacity to present an alternative to the current unrestrained consumerism that has characterized the world in recent times. The rediscovery of the simple life by redirecting human attention toward important lives reduces consumerism thus making the world more sustainable and equal besides making the planet a better place to live in. So, in the face of the challenges of the upcoming years, the minimalistic way of life characterized with the purpose, thoughtfulness, and wise choice may turn out to be the most effective weapon in creating a world that is more harmonious and balanced.

Minimalism, as perspicuous in the future, remains loose and can be adapted into a dynamic philosophy that can be thrived as per the needs of a future world. Its primary values being that of being present, uncluttered, and having a laser focus on essential virtues serve as a rich blueprint for contemporary society. The earth as a planet, the microeconomic conditions within societies, or the global issues that we face, whichever level you take, the minimalist approach of raising efficiency through less and less can be a sustainable way of the near future.

Conclusion: Embracing the Beauty of Simplicity

As we reach the conclusion of this journey through the principles and practices of minimalism, it is time to reflect on the transformation that this lifestyle offers. Minimalism is more than just a method for decluttering or a trend in modern living; it is a profound shift in perspective that invites us to reconsider our relationship with the material world and, ultimately, with ourselves. Throughout this book, we have explored the many facets of minimalism, from its philosophical roots to its practical applications in daily life. We have delved into the psychological benefits, the challenges of adopting this lifestyle in a consumer-driven society, and the long-term impact of living with less but gaining so much more.

The journey of minimalism is one of continuous growth and self-discovery. It is a path that encourages us to strip away the non-essential, not just in our physical spaces but also in our minds and hearts. By focusing on what truly matters, we open up space for deeper connections, more meaningful experiences, and a clearer sense of purpose. Minimalism is not about deprivation or sacrifice; it is about reclaiming our time, energy, and attention from the distractions of modern life and redirecting them towards the things that bring us genuine joy and fulfillment.

As you reflect on the ideas and insights shared in this book, it is important to recognise that minimalism is not a destination but a journey. It is an evolving process that adapts to the different stages and circumstances of our lives. What minimalism looks like for you today may change as you grow, as your values shift, and as you encounter new experiences. The key takeaway is that minimalism is a tool for intentional living, one that empowers you to make choices that align with your deepest values and aspirations.

I encourage you to continue exploring and refining your minimalist lifestyle. Embrace the process of regularly reassessing your possessions, habits, and commitments. Stay curious about new ways to simplify and streamline your life, and remain open to the possibilities that minimalism can create. Whether it's deepening your relationships, pursuing passions that bring you joy, or finding peace in the everyday moments, minimalism can be a powerful catalyst for personal growth and transformation.

In my own journey, I have found that minimalism is not just about the external act of letting go but also about the internal shift towards a life of greater clarity, contentment, and purpose. It has taught me that true wealth is not measured by what we own but by the richness of our experiences, the depth of our connections, and the joy we find in simplicity. Minimalism has helped me to focus on what truly matters, to cultivate gratitude for the present moment, and to live with a sense of intentionality that brings both peace and fulfillment.

As you move forward, I encourage you to embrace the beauty of simplicity in all its forms. Let minimalism be a guide that helps you navigate the complexities of modern life with grace and clarity. Allow it to lead you towards a life that is not just free from excess but filled with meaning, purpose, and joy. Remember that the essence of minimalism is not about having less but about making room for more—more of what brings you happiness, more of what nourishes your soul, and more of what aligns with the person you aspire to be.

Thank you for joining me on this journey through the art of living simply. I hope that the insights and practices shared in this book have inspired you to embark on your own path of minimalism and that you find the joy and fulfillment that come with living a life of intentionality and purpose. As you continue on this journey, may you discover the true abundance that lies in simplicity, and may you live each day with a heart full of gratitude and a life rich in meaning.

About the Author

Evelyn Hartwell is a passionate advocate for intentional living and simplicity. With a deep interest in philosophy, happiness, and the art of minimalism, Evelyn has dedicated herself to exploring how we can cultivate a life of greater clarity, purpose, and joy. Joy in Simplicity: Embracing Minimalism for a Happier Life is her debut book, inspired by her own journey towards a more meaningful and fulfilling existence. Through her writing, Evelyn seeks to inspire others to find the beauty in living with less and to discover the profound impact that minimalism can have on every aspect of life. She believes that true happiness is found not in the accumulation of things but in the richness of our experiences and the connections we nurture. Evelyn lives with her family in a cozy home, where she continues to practice and refine the principles of minimalism in her everyday life.

www.ingramcontent.com/pod-product-compliance
Lightning Source LLC
La Vergne TN
LVHW091457170726
843492LV00001B/223